'The special quality of Drabble's writing is that he is sympathetic to wild life without ever being sentimental'

Birmingham Evening Mail

'A practical book, set down in a straightforward way, yet taking the reader into the very heart of the countryside and introducing him to the wildlife which can be found there'

The Dalesman

'Mr Drabble sets his scene with deft touches'

Country Life

'He writes attractively, with a knack of bringing a breath of country air to his pages'

Manchester Evening News

Also by Phil Drabble in Sphere Books:

COUNTRY SEASONS
ONE MAN AND HIS DOG

Country Scene

PHIL DRABBLE

Photographs by Stanley Porter

SPHERE BOOKS LIMITED

SPHERE BOOKS LTD

Penguin Books Ltd, 27 Wrights Lane, London w8 5tz (Publishing and Editorial)
and Harmondsworth, Middlesex, England (Distribution and Warehouse)
Viking Penguin Inc., 40 West 23rd Street, New York, New York 10010, USA
Penguin Books Australia Ltd, Ringwood, Victoria, Australia
Penguin Books Canada Ltd, 2801 John Street, Markham, Ontario, Canada l3r 1b4
Penguin Books (NZ) Ltd, 182–190 Wairau Road, Auckland 10, New Zealand

First published in Great Britain by Pelham Books Ltd, 1974
Published by Sphere Books Ltd 1978
Reissued 1988

Made and printed in Great Britain by
Richard Clay Ltd, Bungay, Suffolk
Set in Intertype Lectura

Contents

Country Scene

1. Romance in eclipse

September 15, 1967

Academic naturalists are often gluttons for toil. They spend whole decades of their lives specialising on one tiny aspect of a single animal or plant or insect. I know a man who keeps a large-scale map of his county. On Saturday and Sunday and every possible evening in the week, he slinks stealthily from his home, lest the family notice his departure.

His map is divided into hundreds of tiny squares. He has spent the last quarter of a century visiting each one in turn. When he gets there, he takes his notebook and pencil and magnifying glass, to make a comprehensive list of every plant he finds. The result is that he has compiled, single-handed, a botanical atlas which shows, at a glance, exactly what flower or plant or bush or tree you will find, if you follow in his footsteps.

This degree of dedication leaves him time for nothing else. My tastes are more catholic, because I like to know a bit about more things than would be possible if I concentrated only on one. I am particularly interested in animal behaviour of any sort.

The other evening, I watched a group of young mammals indulging in what, I am sure, the zoologists would analyse as courtship displays. They split into pairs and performed a peculiar sort of dance with no perceptible rhythm. Sometimes, two would shuffle together and then part company, jerking and swinging in an arc, until they met again. Their posture was upright, but it might have been difficult for any but the experts to have been sure of their sex. They were immature specimens of the species *Homo sapiens vulgaris*. They were the young of Common Man.

Watching these young folk dance, I amused myself in speculation about what the scientists' reaction would be to the same behaviour in any other species. They would read ponderous papers to learned societies. They would propound abstruse theories to explain plumage, called 'gear', and their song from which all melody had been ousted by noise.

I care less for such high falutin theories than for the enjoyment of what I see. Because I live among wild creatures, I appreciate the commonplace as much as rarity.

Outside my study window, as I write, a pair of tufted ducks are conspiring to seduce me from my desk. They are tempting me out to the rain-washed turf, brilliantly green in the watery autumn sun. The motive for their display is no complicated reflex. They simply know that, when I emerge, a bowl of appetising corn will not be far away.

The duck is dowdy blackish-brown. Although her legs and bill are a subtle bluey-grey, you can only see this at close quarters. She has a startlingly yellow eye. Her mate is much the same, and they move, on land, with the rolling gait of full-bellied sailors.

You see best the magic of these 'tufties' only when they are afloat. One second they bob about, unsinkable as corks, the next they have sunk without trace. Seconds later, they reappear, yards away, sleek and unruffled as the rabbit from the conjuror's hat.

Even on land, they are only dull for a while. Although their plumage is in eclipse now, the drake's dark feathers will soon moult out, to leave flanks and belly and wing-bars an iridescent white. This will contrast with his shining blacks to make him show up as vivid as a magpie. To round off the outfit, he will be crowned with a crest, or tuft, of showy black feathers. The sleek formality of human evening dress is seedy by comparison.

Nevertheless, he looks a mess at the moment. His plumage, halfway betwixt a duck's dull brown and a drake's flamboyance, labels him a hermaphrodite – wildew, as the locals call him. But when he changes out of eclipse, he'll stay gorgeous till summer comes again.

His extrovert virility will capture the heart of the demurest duck on the pool, and he'll sire the ducklings in the eggs she lays. The odds against the survival of these defenceless ducklings are terrifying. So Nature has been lavish enough to allow some over for hard lines.

The first clutch of eggs is often laid early, when the grass and leaves have not grown thick enough to hide them. Except in very forward seasons, these are usually eaten by crows or jays or magpies or rats. Luckily, this often happens before the poor duck has had time to complete her clutch. It isn't terribly serious then, because she'll keep on trying, in another nest, until she has laid as many eggs as she can cover.

When she has completed her clutch, she 'feathers her nest'.

She plucks tiny feathers from her breast, to make an eider-down to cover her eggs every time she leaves them. Not only does this prevent them from getting chilled while she is away feeding, it also hides them from the prying eyes of predators.

Even so, the odds against survival may force her to lay two or three clutches before she hatches young successfully. The drake does his bit unwittingly. There is no point in being attractive when the ducks lose interest, so he sheds his bright colours, and moults into eclipse once more. He ceases to be a bright target to attract the attention of any enemy in sight.

The experts may consider my little tufties too common to notice and the mechanism of their eclipse elementary stuff. But it still spells romance for me.

2. Odds against the deer

October 13, 1967

It was a shock when a farmer told me that he had shot between thirty-five and forty wild fallow deer, during the last twelve months, on his farm on the edge of Cannock Chase. This wholesale destruction of one of the largest and most beautiful wild animals still roaming free in England raises the whole question of our responsibility to wild life.

A century ago a thousand deer were said to roam over the sixteen square miles of the Chase. In those days, it was split up into great estates, and farmers were tenants who would have been evicted if they had shot a pheasant, far less a deer. There were few visitors to disturb the peace.

During the wars when food was scarce, a tasty dish of venison was worth the risk of poaching. The Forestry Commission took over about half the land for woodland in the 1920s and their policy was to eradicate anything which damaged trees, including deer. So there was no deer problem until after the war.

Then the policy of the Commission changed and they appointed a Game Warden whose job it was to conserve deer, instead of killing them indiscriminately. When it was necessary to thin out any, they were carefully selected so that the quality of the remainder was improved by scientific selection of the breeding stock. Numbers swelled and spilled out on to the open Chase, where they had been rare for years before.

Meanwhile, about five square miles of land had come under the control of Staffordshire County Council, who take great pride in administering it for the benefit of the public. They declared a central area of about 1,000 acres to be a Motorless Zone for those who loved grand scenery and wild places and were prepared to walk to fill their city lungs with clean fresh air.

This was fine for the public but not so good for the deer. Predictably, they took flight from barking dogs and gales of happy laughter. Between the public access zone and the farmland above the River Trent, there is an area of mature hardwood. Generations of deer have wandered for miles in autumn,

12

to gorge on the chestnuts and acorns there, so that it was the perfect refuge to seek when the public flooded on to their feeding grounds. Naturally, they were unwilling to venture out again on to the land from which they had been disturbed. They tried their luck instead on the farmland on the other side of the fence.

This farm is also controlled by the County Council and their tenant is the man who told me that he has shot two score deer this year.

Before your anger swells, consider his plight. His living is wrung from the land. Deer are destructive to his potatoes and too many deer trample on his corn as well. He estimates that the damage done by those which survived his barrage is between £200 and £300 this year. It is easy for us to cast stones when he is left to foot the bill.

Nor is the public blameless. The wardens who work for the County Council and the Forestry Commission collected, between them, about another forty deer which had been killed by motorists, despite the warning notices requesting care. This brings the total to around eighty deer which died last year for raiding crops or when they were crossing roads.

The Council warden estimates the herd size as one hundred and fifty. To keep that number static, without increase or decrease, only one in six, or twenty-five in all, could be spared in any year. So the present rate of slaughter, if it continues, spells inevitable disaster.

Gerald Springthorpe, the Forestry Game Warden, is an acknowledged expert on fallow deer, and trains officers in deer management from all over the country. A stroll with him in Commission woodlands shows that the deer on the Chase have not been driven out of the woodland by lack of food. They are browsing creatures which do not graze close like sheep, but feed on bilberry and bramble, birch and the wide variety of plants that grow on forest rides. You can see more in an hour on forest land than in half a day in the Motorless Zone.

Mr Springthorpe is planting 'deer lawns' in quiet areas, undisturbed by the public, to attract 'his' deer away from danger. But that is not enough.

Sir Charles Wolseley, a neighbouring landowner, has joined with the Commission to erect a fence, more than two miles long, to protect the farmland which is especially vulnerable because unusual concentrations of deer congregate there.

When I was investigating this problem, a senior Planning

Officer said that his responsibility was to people not animals. I disagree. I do not believe that we have the right to drug wood pigeons with narcotics, as Worcestershire farmers want to do. I believe that we should give otters and badgers and deer, all of which would face extinction through our actions, the same protection the law has given to threatened birds for years. And I think we should also protect the people who would suffer as a result.

The British Deer Society has offered to erect a fence free if the Council will buy the materials. They know that only this will save the deer on Cannock Chase from the righteous wrath of aggrieved farmers. I hope public opinion may force the Council to act while there are yet some deer to save.

3. Witness to murder

October 27, 1967

I feel indirectly responsible for the death of the neatest and most dapper pied wagtail I ever saw. He was a favourite bird of mine and I would never have done him intentional harm, but I realised too late that I could easily have averted his death – and I still have a guilty conscience about it.

It happened last spring. We were sitting by the window watching a pair of wagtails catching flies on the lawn. Although we were only a few feet away, they took not the slightest notice.

Their colours were more subdued than a magpie's brash black and white. Nevertheless, the smart black crown and throat and the whiter than white underside, made them stand out in any company. Once the cock came so close to the window that I could see the pupil in his dark eye, and he so shone with health that there wasn't a feather out of place.

Both of them caught an occasional fly in mid-air as adroitly as a flycatcher, but they were even more spectacular on the ground. Their long tails flicked up and down to get precise balance and direction. Then, a bird that was yards away one second, had scooped up the fly the next. Their strides were so rapid that their feet were as blurred with movement as the blades of a fan – and the finest ballet dancer was sluggish and graceless by comparison.

We saw the cock bird fly to the far end of the lawn, swooping and chattering at something hidden from us behind a rhododendron. We wondered if it was a rival wagtail. Whatever it was, it was moving through the plants, along the flower bed, towards the window.

The hen bird left her flycatching too and joined in the row, egging her old man on to more abuse. His fury rose to an uninhibited crescendo. He dived and chattered until, at last, a weasel darted from the cover of a plant to the safety of a crevice under the step. We took off our hats to the courage of the bird and practically booed the villain, who had been so routed by our hero.

Right triumphs in the wild as rarely as in our pseudocivilised society. Within seconds, a snakelike head poked out of hiding to see where the hecklers had gone. The coast, for the moment, was clear and the weasel came out again onto the lawn. The wagtails returned to the attack and we noticed that they were not as foolish as they looked. Whatever threats they used, they never went quite close enough for the weasel to grab them.

He knew this perfectly well and he somersaulted and chased his tail, and rolled and tumbled about, always in retreat. His antics gave the birds a false sense of security and they became more and more intoxicated by their sense of victory. He fooled them, and I admit he fooled us too. I know now that I should have opened the window and clapped my hands and the weasel would have been in the next parish in no time at all.

But I was enthralled by the drama and wanted a seat in the stalls to watch the hero vanquish the villain in real life. Real life is not so cosy. The weasel gradually gambolled closer and closer to a clump of bushes and the wagtails grew bolder and bolder as they put him to flight. He disappeared under the cover of some leaves for a fraction of a second, and the cock bird followed to see where he had gone.

He hadn't gone at all. He was waiting for that one false move – and with a flurry of ruffled feathers, it was all over. We were almost as stunned as the victim.

Superstition says that all wagtails have a drop of Devil's blood in their veins. That is because of their black and white colouring which is associated with evil. Perhaps there is something in it after all, because the hen was a widow for too short a time for decency.

Within a few days, another dapper cock had taken her under his wing and they commenced to build a nest in the garage, almost before the weasel had time to digest the old man. They reared two families and now they have gone.

In winter, pied wagtails often congregate in enormous communal roosts, and one of these is in the very heart of Birmingham. It is in the ventilators of a roof over furnaces where lead is melted to make car batteries. Dr Clive Minton, the ornithologist, took me there and we counted about 1,500 birds, in tidy rows, like pigeons in a pigeon loft.

Their roost was warm all right, but smoky too, so they were as dowdy as town sparrows. To make things worse, they have to fly miles, every day, over the city to get to their feeding grounds. If 'our' birds are among that lot, I hope that they will smarten themselves up before they come back to our lawn next spring.

4. Milk bottle death traps

November 10, 1967

An empty milk bottle may appear to be an unconventional place to photograph a common shrew (see centre section). A dead shrew with its feet forlornly pawing the air may well seem an odd subject to choose for a portrait at all. It is a photograph that never would have been if it was not for an unknown litter-lout. If he sees it, I hope it will give him a guilty conscience.

Alongside almost every lay-by, on every main road, there is an accumulation of dangerous rubbish. Indigestible plastic bags that can kill cows that eat them, rusty tins to cut their feet and broken glass to start fires by concentrating the rays of the sun.

But I confess it had never occurred to me until a year or so ago that perfectly sound empty bottles were particularly dangerous. I was attending a conference of the Mammal Society and had listened to a series of highly scientific lectures that any but the most dedicated naturalist might have considered academic and dull.

Then two young men got up and began to describe a most unconventional method of assessing the population of a whole range of small mammals. Wherever they went, they said, they kept their eyes skinned for empty bottles lying on their sides. Their most fruitful hunting grounds were the lay-bys along unattractive main roads.

This was no leg-pull. The two learned young beach-combers had almost literally stumbled on a brand-new method of taking a census of small creatures that are normally difficult to assess. Mice and voles and shrews are very curious, and are driven by compulsion to explore any hole or crevice that they find on their travels. This is sensible enough, because if a cat or owl or hawk appears unexpectedly, it may be a matter of life or death to know the nearest safe hiding-place.

If an empty milk bottle is lying conveniently on its side in grass or nettles, the local mouse population will automatically pop in to explore. It is usually the last thing they do. They slither down the neck all right, but their leathery little feet cannot get enough grip on the slippery glass to climb out again.

When the next mammalogist comes by he will make a note

of the species and number he finds and transfer them – as statistics – to his mammal-census forms. The odds are that only a small percentage of the readers of this column have ever seen a live shrew similar to the one in the photograph before he got into the bottle. Based on the statistics compiled by the scientists, this is very surprising because shrews are so common that they inhabit almost every rough patch of grass and bramble, the bottoms of hedgerows and even urban gardens.

Although most people would mistake them for mice, they are really more nearly related to hedgehogs and moles. Indeed, their snouts are very pointed and mole-like and they have the canine teeth of all carnivorous animals instead of rodents' chisels designed for gnawing grain.

They do man nothing but good, living exclusively on a flesh diet, mostly insects and worms, and they never blot their copybooks by eating so much as a garden pea or grain of corn. Perhaps it is because they do live in such thick cover and are hard to see that they have been so misunderstood and so persecuted through the ages.

The Romans thought their bite was deadly dangerous and 'shrew-struck' has become another name for paralysis. Teeth that have been feeding on flesh and are as sharp as hypodermic needles are not the most sterile instruments to choose for an inoculation. Perhaps the Romans were right! This ancient belief of dangerous paralysis after the bite of a shrew persisted down the ages.

It was recounted by Dr Robert Plot who wrote a fascinating history of Staffordshire in 1686, and by the Rev. Gilbert White, who was telling exactly the same story almost a century later in his *Natural History of Selborne*. They both believed that lameness in cattle was caused by the animals being bitten by the shrew-mouse, as White called it, or a nurse-row as it was known in Plot's day. They even went so far as to believe that if a shrew so much as ran across the flank of a cow without biting it at all, the cow would go lame.

The cure that was prescribed was to apply twigs from a 'shrew-ash' to the affected limb. A shrew-ash was produced by man. A hole was bored with an augur to the centre of the tree and a live shrew was popped in. Before he had time to escape, the hole was plugged with wood from the same tree to entomb him for ever. This, it was thought, gave the tree supernatural powers of healing which would last as long as the tree lived.

18

Thereafter, the twigs were a certain cure for shrew-struck cattle.

All this happened less than a couple of hundred years ago. In your great grandfather's time, if you happen to come from a long-lived family. But don't let's get too smug about how much better we are now.

First, consider the modern word 'shrewd'. My dictionary says that it means 'penetrating' or 'astute'. It also says 'malicious' or 'scolding'. Quite a contradiction, you might think, until you remember great grandfather's theories about paralysis. To do a shrewd deal you paralyse your opponent with your astuteness. If you fail, you paralyse him with the malicious eloquence of your tongue.

5. Bats in the belfry

December 1, 1967

The keenest bell ringers lose their zeal if there is a flock of pigeons roosting in the rafters. Our bell ringers have recently solved the trouble by nailing wire netting over every possible point of entry into the belfry. Quite large mesh netting would have kept the pigeons and jackdaws and starlings out, but exponents of any craft do like to make doubly sure that whatever job they do is done thoroughly.

The netting they used was only half-an-inch across each mesh. It would keep out not only birds but is small enough to exclude almost anything bigger than a bumble bee. The result, I am sorry to say, is that we have no more bats in our belfry. This is a pity because I think bats are an asset in any church.

Not only do they sometimes enliven even the longest sermon by hawking insects in the rafters, but they are the most effective enemies of woodworm and death-watch beetles. The grubs that eat their way into wood leaving their tunnels as evidence are safe enough. But when they develop into adult beetles they have to emerge to breed, and a flourishing colony of bats will mop them up as fast as they come out before they have even had time to make a date.

Many of our most ancient buildings and churches stood firm and sound down the centuries with no sign of decaying woodwork. Then, quite suddenly, within the last few generations, death-watch beetle and woodworm moved in.

I have a theory about this that is impossible to prove. I believe that the trouble started when the gargoyles that cascaded water off the roof were replaced by guttering and downspouts. We began to grow effete and put heating systems into churches. To make the best of them, we blocked up all the holes and crevices to keep the heat in. By doing so, we kept the bats out and allowed death-watch beetles to crawl about the roof and breed with impunity.

Although it may be desirable to prevent birds from roosting and nesting inside buildings, I do think it commonsense to leave room for a few bats to prey on the insects that ravage the rafters.

Some people have an instinctive aversion to bats. Last summer, I was in a lamp-lit marquee enjoying the tail-end of a wedding reception, when a long-eared bat flew in. The effect was dramatic. Within seconds, about half the women had disappeared with their hands clasped over their heads. The idea that bats entangle themselves in women's hair is absolute nonsense, but it did leave us more room to enjoy a superb display of aerobatics.

Even scientists are less than fair to them. For centuries bats were creatures of nocturnal mystery and then quite suddenly at the end of the last war they became the objects of concentrated scientific investigation. It became fashionable to take up 'bat banding' or 'bat ringing'.

Scientists searched for colonies of bats that roosted by day in caves and buildings and old quarry or mine workings. They found them there hanging upside down and fitted numbered metal bands to what corresponds to our forearms. A ring can be seen on the long-eared bat in the illustration in the centre of the book.

These rings start as bands with a gap wide enough to slide over the bat's forearm. The ring is then closed on like a single handcuff. The ring is as light and as free from sharp edges as possible. It is numbered so that anyone finding that bat again can report the place and time so that information about movement and life span can be compiled.

Many people will be surprised that there are more than a dozen species of bat in England. They range in size from the tiny Pipistrelle or flitter mouse with a wing span of seven inches or so, to Noctules whose wing spans up to fifteen inches.

A great deal of the early work was done on the Greater Horseshoe bat that commonly roosts in caves and old tin workings in Devonshire. They roost in colonies that are fairly accessible and continuous observation has been kept on them for more than ten years. Because of their numbered rings, they are known as individuals. Scientists have weighed them and measured them, recorded their pregnancies and the number of their young.

They have discovered the same bats in places many miles apart, and have begun to plot the pattern of their migrations. They discovered at what time they hibernated and how much weight they lost. They tabulated their food from analysis of their droppings and have even listed the fleas that suck their blood.

But for me the most important discovery they have made is that the numbered bands, the key to the whole operation, sometimes cause discomfort to the bats. If they are too thin, they irritate them, and the bat's strong teeth may crush the ring tighter on to its forearm. If they are too thick, they are heavy and more difficult to apply gently. In dark caves moisture sometimes condenses on them and softens the tender flesh beneath.

Scientists are well aware of this and are trying to devise some more simple form of identification that will cause less discomfort. Meanwhile, they examine every bat they catch for signs of irritation and remove the ring if necessary. They try to discourage students and research workers from doing short-term projects and then leaving the bats they have marked to take their chance, instead of observing them regularly to see nothing goes wrong.

It is a depressing catalogue of disadvantage for the bat to weigh against the luxury of enlarged human academic learning. I wish the boffins would learn to observe them without any interference at all.

6. Red rags to bulls and badgers

December 8, 1967

The story that bulls are so susceptible to colour that if you wave a red flag at one he will inevitably attack you, is an old wives' tale. If he happens to be that sort of bull, the colour of your rag would make no difference at all. You would invite trouble as soon as he saw you.

I do not mean that all bulls are fierce. Bulls of dairy breeds, black-and-white Friesians or Short-horns, are usually worse than those of the beef breeds, like Herefords. Jersey and Guernsey bulls, from the Channel Isles, are often so aggressive that it takes two men to pilot one small bull round the arena of an agricultural show.

Longhorn cattle, on the other hand, are famous for superb, slow-growing beef, and their formidable horns often span more than five feet. They are usually as docile as old ladies at a bridge party.

But no bull of any breed is really to be trusted, even without a red rag. Only fools and professional bull fighters take any chances with them. Whatever the truth about red rags and bulls, there is no doubt that tearing cloth is irresistible to some other animals.

The men who race whippets have exploited this for generations. They begin by waving a duster near a litter of puppies. The whippet pups examine the cloth, just as they investigate anything else that moves. They find it soft and pliant to play with and soon start a tug-of-war. Within seconds their docility shells off and they become fierce, primeval hunters, tearing at their prey.

By the time they have developed into lithe, sinewy running dogs, they are obsessed by the illusion that a waving rag is their natural quarry and their subsequent training encourages their belief with great artistry.

A young dog is led by his trainer, who holds him at one end of a field. He takes a firm grip at the base of the dog's tail, with one hand. With the other, he grasps the scruff of its neck equally firmly. Using a sledgehammer to crack a nut, you might think, for whippets are gentle little dogs and such a grip would pin a wild fox to immobility. The reason is obvious as soon as the owner pulls a rag from his pocket. The dog goes mad to get at it, writhing and squirming and snapping to break free.

As if this was not enough, the owner incites it to further frenzy by waving his rag like a second in the boxing-ring, while he backs away across the field, yelling encouragement all the time. When, at last, they are a measured 200 yards apart, the whippet is loosed. He streaks off, to leap the last few paces, catching the waving rag in mid air and clinging on to it with the tenacity of a bulldog.

Whippet racing 'to the rag' is simply an extension of this, when a number of dogs are loosed simultaneously to race to their owners, who stand yelling and waving cloths at the far end of the track. The competitive atmosphere and indescribable hub-bub excite the dogs. But it is the prospect of the limp surrender of that tearing cloth which draws out the last ounce of effort.

There may not seem much similarity between the sprightly daintiness of fine-drawn whippets and the ruthless attacks of Alsatian guard dogs, but the initial part of their training is basically the same. Alsatians, too, are loosed to chase a piece of cloth, which is waved by a retreating trainer pretending to be an escaping crook. The dog doesn't regard him as such. It is just a game to him, with a rag to tear as first prize.

When the dog gets really enthusiastic, the trainer puts on a thick leather gauntlet and wraps the rag round that. The next time the dog grabs hold, he is unaware in the excitement that he has grabbed a mouthful of arm as well. He will soon chase anyone who runs and grab his arm – whether it is padded or not – and hold him powerless until his trainer comes.

It is not easy to discover if wild animals would experience the same kicks by ripping cloth as domestic animals do. Quite recently, Stanley Porter unwittingly provided a clue. He has spent his leisure for years photographing wildlife and this summer and autumn he kept a portable hide at Goat Lodge. He left it set up for photographing herons and the next time we visited it, it was more than dilapidated.

At first I blamed our roebuck. When their antlers are growing to maturity, deer fray off the velvet covering on saplings, which they thrash until the tree is killed. I wondered if a photographic hide was a more satisfying victim to conquer. In the end we discovered the real culprit – and got photographic evidence to prove it.

It turned out to be the badger I had hand-reared this spring, who now lives at complete liberty in a sett in the paddock, as free to come and go as any wild badger. When he discovered what fun it was to knock hell out of cloth on an inanimate frame, he turned his attention on the trouser turn-ups on my more animate legs!

Next summer, Stanley Porter hopes to move his hide to the open wood, outside, where there are plenty of wild badgers. If they are fired by the same ambition, he will either have to wear shorts or buy a suit of armour.

7. The credit side of snow

December 15, 1967

The roebuck outside my study window was searching for any grains of maize the pigeons had left. He sauntered quietly along, head hung low, testing the air with his sensitive nose for the faintest aroma of food. Suddenly, he froze into immobility except for one foreleg that swung rapidly, apparently as compulsively as a water diviner's wand. It scattered flurries of snow and exposed the turf beneath. The buck nuzzled delightedly around, picking up the individual grains of corn he'd uncovered.

If this portrait had appeared on a Christmas card, I might have suspected that the artist had dipped too deeply into the well of imaginative licence. It is very rare indeed to see roebucks with antlers against a background of snow. Their old antlers normally fall off about the third week in November and the new ones do not grow until the beginning of the breeding season next spring.

One man's meat is another man's poison. While our buck was demonstrating his capacity for coping with wintry conditions, the same few inches of snow had brought urban traffic to a standstill. Miles of commuter cars had snarled up into inextricable cats-cradles. Trains ran with no heating and some not at all, tempers frayed and inflated the skithering of snow to a national disaster.

From the objective isolation of deep country, this mountain shrank to molehill proportions. I took a huge bass broom and swept paths through the snow from the back door to the lane outside, and to the tractor shed where we keep a few logs dry. I brushed snow off the old millstone that the birds use as their canteen and I replenished their larder with scraps of fat and cheese and a bucketful of sweepings from the floor of the local cornmill.

By the time I'd taken the dogs for a sharp walk to the farmland at the other end of the wood, my hands were warm enough to set about the chores of melting the ice in poultry troughs and giving them clean water. The snow, sufficient for all that city fuss, had not even covered the woodland floor, so I scattered wheat for the fowls on a carpet of leaves. Scientific

26

poultry keepers would say that I was wasting good food to keep up the body heat of hens that should have been indoors, converting the same energy to eggs. But I like my eggs fresh from fowls that are healthy with natural living. Comparing their lot to that of their cousins cramped in battery cages, I thought they'd probably agree.

Then I left the dogs in the house and went for a walk by myself. I went alone because I wanted to see exactly what had crossed our land, without the complications of additional footprints of four energetic dogs. There were far fewer grey squirrel marks than I had feared, perhaps because they were lying snug and warm in the holes hollowed in oak trees by green woodpeckers. And there were far more hares than I dared to hope.

A neighbouring shooting syndicate had shot thirty-six on one day in September and I knew there were very few left on the farmland. The evidence of footprints in the snow showed that the woodland hares, feeding on less attractive forage than clover in stubble or corn on plough, had more than held their own.

I found the footprints of two stoats and a weasel and a colony of rats that had taken up residence in some straw bales where I feed the birds. I saw lots of tiny tracks made by voles and shrews and long-tailed woodmice that might seem too much like fairies to leave any marks at all.

The thing that really shook me, though, was the evidence of foxes. There are a thousand acres of Forestry Commission woods right next door to us. This forest merges with Marchington Woodlands which, in turn, join up with what remains of Needwood Forest. It is, by Midland standards, an enormous area of woodland and would inevitably hold a fair few foxes.

But there did seem to be more foxes than anything else. They didn't wander about feeding haphazardly as the hares did. Most of them seemed to come in on one side of our wood and follow well defined 'runs' or paths that led directly out on the other side. There is a boundary fence of wire netting to keep cattle from surrounding farms out of the wood. The fox runs converged on the ditches where they could pass under this netting. I noted where they went for future reference.

It was obvious that they were travelling from dense cover, where they could lie-up safely by day, to their feeding grounds. To the small pools where they could catch the odd waterhen, or marshy clumps where pheasants roosted.

And at this time of year, dog foxes will often travel further in search of love than food. Four miles away on the other side of the forest there were farms where cattle had been slaughtered because of foot-and-mouth disease. I wondered how many of the foxes that cross our wood had been there first.

The snow that disclosed the secrets of these vagabonds may also help to combat the dreaded plague. Although foot-and-mouth disease can withstand great cold, the snow at least covers it temporarily. It may well swill into crevices in the ground and die when the thaw comes.

So this snow, which caused such chaos in busy towns, did little harm to us but made us work a bit harder to keep warm. The cattle plague, looming blacker in the country than dock strikes or devaluations, means to many townsmen that they can't go fishing or ski-ing or hiking.

Strange how unimportant the other fellows' troubles can seem.

8. Saving the birds from their friends

January 19, 1968

The Protection of Birds Act, 1967, which received the Royal Assent last July, became law this week. A Bewick swan flew into an electric power line and broke a wing a year ago, and has settled down happily with me, living on my pool. But it is one of the rare birds that this Act now specially protects and I am not quite certain if I would have committed an offence, had the new Act been in force at the time, by caging it while it got well.

You certainly need a licence from the National Environment Research Council now, even to photograph a sitting corncrake, disturb a red-necked phalarope at her nest, or put a ring on the leg of a wryneck. These, and a great many other birds, are specially protected.

You are unlikely to commit any of these offences unless you belong to a highly specialist minority of academic ornithologists. Nevertheless, the reason why it became desirable to pass such an Act is very significant.

It has been necessary, in the past, to legislate for the protection of rare birds and their eggs from sportsmen and collectors, for the simple reason that otherwise, the only rare birds we could see would be stuffed in glass cases. But the 1967 Protection of Birds Act is aimed not at people who want to kill birds for sport, collect them like rare stamps, or even to use their flamboyant feathers to furnish ladies' hats.

This is an Act that is not directed at people who like birds too little, but at those who love them too much. Natural History programmes on radio and television often attract big audiences. Once a thirst for knowledge about the countryside has been fired, its flame is fanned by a profusion of books and articles and magazines. It is thus easy enough to become an armchair naturalist, but the urge to put one's theories to the test is then likely to become compulsive.

This is easy enough, too. Leisure has escalated until working hours demand less than half our waking life. The days when an expedition into the country was an adventure, needing careful planning and tedious waits for buses, have long been left behind by the motor car. Nowadays, carloads of dedicated bird watchers are decanted into the countryside every weekend and, at first, they are fully content to do little but stand and stare.

They have learned to identify birds and animals and plants and insects from still pictures in books, and the dull flatness of the little screen. Suddenly, these portraits spring to life in 3-D, and it becomes exciting to return home in the evening and distil the intimate details of their lives from the written word. The better educated we become, the less we are satisfied by being spectators, and the more we yearn to take an active part ourselves.

It suddenly seems more satisfying to make an original personal discovery, however insignificant, than to read about the most important research by someone else. As a result, the swelling nostalgia for country things has deluged the countryside with people, no longer content with the satisfaction of enjoying things in lovely places.

They want, instead, to do something positive. To count the numbers and varieties of ducks on a reservoir or to take photographs better than anyone else has taken before. And some crave to probe the secrets of birds' lives by fixing rings to their legs and recording their movements.

One of the less attractive facets of our modern society is that it is bitterly competitive. Unfortunately, this trait spills over into our pastimes as badly as our work. It appears more thrilling to fix a ring on a rarity or to compile statistics on something that has never been investigated before; not because it is intrinsically better, but because it is different.

So the pressure upon the creatures in the countryside is not evenly distributed. People want to watch or photograph or ring the few rare birds, not the multitude of common ones. The easiest way to study them is usually at their nest because their maternal instinct makes them unnaturally bold. But, if she is disturbed too frequently or roughly, even the bravest mother will eventually desert her eggs or young.

It is not only cruel to make her do this, but, when a crop of youngsters is destroyed, the survivors become even more rare and so are subject to even greater pressure.

So this new Act makes it an offence to disturb any wild bird on Schedule One while it is at or near a nest containing eggs or unfledged young, without a licence. (The law makes exceptions for species unlucky enough to be regarded as harmful.)

If you want a licence, you must apply to the Natural Environment Research Council. Before they will grant permission to disturb a rare bird (listed in Schedule One of the Act) they will require you to fill in a form. You will have to state why you want to disturb the bird at all, and give very full details, where you want to do it, and what species you want to study. You have to say who else will be there, your previous experience, the equipment you want to use, and how long the work will take. Finally, you have to give the names of two referees to vouch for what you say.

I loathe bureaucracy in general and form-filling in particular. But at least this Act is being taken seriously, for I know of one very reputable person who has applied and had his form smartly returned because he only supplied one referee. So I welcome the Act, because, though it erodes our liberty a little more, it should at least curb intrusion harmful to our rarer birds.

I hope there will be more Acts like it, to limit the ill effects of more and more people converging on fewer and fewer quiet and lonely places that we should preserve as sanctuaries for birds instead of bird watchers.

9. The ferret that went to a dance

February 2, 1968

When I bought my first ferret, more than forty years ago, it was a major victory over the family. They had fought a long, defensive war to prevent any confrontation between a ferret and me. They said that ferrets stank; that they were incurably savage; that they would escape and kill the neighbour's poultry. None of this was inevitable. Their one trump card was: 'Who is going to look after it, while you are away at school?'

So I directed a treacly stream of charm at my headmaster. I tried to persuade him that the education of his pupils was scarcely complete until they knew how to provide their own amusement, by ferreting rabbits, or as a service to the community by catching rats.

You don't catch old birds with chaff, so I was brushed off there, too.

Then Hairy Kelly, our local rat catcher, came to my rescue by offering to look after a ferret for me while I was away. The financial arrangements are best forgotten for I should have been on a better thing if I had given him the ferret outright at the end of the holidays and bought another when I came home again. But I felt it worth being played for a mug for the psychological luxury of kicking away the last plank of my parents' opposition.

I kept ferrets continuously after that, until rabbits were wiped out by myxomatosis. I bred ferrets, bought ferrets, sold ferrets and used them for ratting and rabbiting.

I even went to a dance with a ferret once. It was some time after the war while petrol could only be used for essential purposes, and there was no valid excuse to take a car half way across the country just to go to a dance. We got round the problem by chucking a ferret, in a bag with some nets, in the back of a car. We then telephoned our rather surprised hostess and declined the invitation to her dance. Instead, we offered to come and catch the rats we were certain infested her fowl-pen. It would be perfectly legal to stay on to the dance, while we were on the spot, and we could tell any policeman who asked us what we were doing so far from home, in evening dress, that we'd only been out ratting! – and produce the ferret as evidence.

Not all my ferrets have been such an unqualified success or displayed such unexpected virtues. Some were as savage as my parents predicted. One of these got such a stranglehold on my forefinger that she converted it from sound flesh to a living pincushion. She drove in four teeth, sharp as red-hot needles, till they met on the bone nine times before I broke free. When the doctor examined those three dozen punctures, he was so impressed that he filled me full of antibiotics until I couldn't be sure which hurt most.

At odd times, my ferrets did escape, and they did kill poultry, though it was usually mine. But, on the whole, they bring back memories that are pleasant and I am sorry there are far fewer ferrets about now than there used to be.

Myxomatosis is a plague as serious for rabbits as foot-and-mouth disease is for cattle. It is no coincidence that the ebbs and flows of rabbit populations are followed by parallel fluctuations in numbers of ferrets. Most people who had ferrets made them earn their keep by catching rabbits for sale. When there were no more rabbits in a district to catch, ferrets were often turned loose to fend for themselves, like stray dogs.

Although it was a practice that I would condemn, a ferret does at least have a better chance of survival than a dog. If it is not caught raiding domestic poultry or pigeons, it may well establish itself where it can catch enough birds or rats or voles to eke out a respectable living. Should it happen to end up in remote country where wild polecats still survive, it will almost certainly cross with them and produce young.

This is not as surprising as it may seem. Ferrets are really domesticated polecats that have been kept in captivity for centuries. White ferrets which have pink eyes are simply albinos, but 'fitchet' ferrets, like the one in the illustration, are practically identical to wild polecats.

Some scientists do claim to be able to tell the difference. They say that the polecat's skull is stouter and stronger than a ferret's. But I have also heard it said that if you rear a litter of 'true' polecats on soft food, and a litter of ferrets on meat, it is the ferrets that grow the stronger skulls. Other scientists will tell you that the guard hairs on a polecat's coat are stiffer and longer. But rats that have constant access to meat in deep freeze, grow abnormally thick fur, so why should not a polecat's thick coat be due to living out in all weathers?

It is, in any case, indisputable that they will interbreed freely. Down the centuries, so many ferrets have been lost rabbiting that I doubt if it is possible to find a pure-blooded polecat anywhere in the British Isles.

Until the war, they were only common in Radnor Forest and round Tregarron Bog in Central Wales. Any that spread further were soon caught by rabbit catchers. Now that gin traps are illegal (except in Scotland, where polecats are virtually extinct) they are spreading to Shropshire and Herefordshire and odd ones farther still.

Whether their pedigrees will bear scrutiny or not, they are almost indistinguishable from the genuine article, and we shall be richer for their presence, so long as their numbers are not allowed to get out of hand.

10. 'A bit of a cripple'

February 16, 1968

Generations of hard and dangerous work have produced a brutal sense of realism in the Black Country. Men who have spent the day manhandling tons of white-hot steel, or hewing coal, half a mile below the earth, do not mince their words nor doll them up to pander to convention.

This fact was indelibly printed on my mind years ago in the bar parlour of a Black Country pub. A huge chain maker elbowed his way across the room, splitting the pall of smoke like a bead curtain. 'Pheel,' he roared, in his Black Country drawl. The hub-bub died as every ear swelled into a trumpet to eavesdrop on what he had to say.

'Pheel, I want you to meet Little 'Arry.' He paused for Little 'Arry to appear. Then he added, 'He's a bit of a cripple.'

It was a glimpse of the obvious and I shuddered for the embarrassment of the poor chap, for his back was cruelly twisted, a legacy of one of his occupational hazards.

I need not have been so squeamish. Constant peril dulls imagination and the bald description meant no more to anyone in that room than if he had been introduced as a glass blower, or a policeman or a collier. This simple fact, which everyone else took in his stride, was an experience which I shall never forget.

So, when a deformed blackbird appeared on our bird table a few weeks ago, it inevitably assumed the title 'Little 'Arry' in memory of the original. His beak was permanently apart and, at first, I thought he was either adenoidal or perpetually on the point of bursting into song. Then I noticed that he never closed his beak at all, not even when he was eating, so I assumed he had suffered some accident.

I have no more inhibitions about prying into the pathological secrets of our visitors than my friends had in that far off Black Country pub. Our bird table is only about six feet from the window and, when I subjected Little 'Arry to scrutiny through a pair of binoculars that magnify the image ten times, he was literally larger than life.

If I had held him in my hands and examined him clinically,

35

his symptoms could have been no clearer. I had assumed that he had had a hairsbreadth escape from a cat or an owl, which had crushed the top mandible of his bill, but had been unable to hang on for the kill. But close examination revealed no scar or other sign of fracture and Stanley Porter, who called to take his portrait, agrees with me that he had probably been 'a bit of a cripple' from birth.

It raised in our minds the question of how he had survived so long, because Nature is normally intolerant of weaklings and they soon go to the wall. The points of his bill are so distorted that it is difficult to imagine how he could grasp the earthworms that form so large a part of blackbirds' bill of fare. So we watched exactly what happened on the bird table.

In the centre, there is a bird-cake. I make it by melting fat in a saucepan and adding household scraps and pellets, so that the birds can't carry them off but have to dine on the table, where we can watch them. There is always a constant procession of visitors and, for the past few weeks, Little 'Arry has been prominent among them.

He predicted the first severe weather more accurately than the Weather Man and made his first appearance in good time to get settled in before the frosts were hard. At that stage, he had no difficulty in stabbing at the soft fat, that stuck in chunks on the point of his bill. A couple of shakes of his head, as a gourmet tosses back oysters, and the fat disappeared. He also scooped down the large grains of whole maize put out for the pigeons, in much the same way.

The wisdom of his timing became obvious when real winter set in. He spent long hours in the paddock, waiting for molehills to rise, hoping to catch the odd worms escaping from the moles below. When the snow covered the hills too deeply, the fat on the bird table froze iron-hard too and he pecked at it incessantly, without any visible effect.

So I mixed him some stiff, warm bread-and-milk and he could barely wait for me to step back before wolfing down great gulps of it. From then on, he never looked back. If he had not had the sense – or the luck, if you don't believe that birds have sense – to come to my bird table, I am certain his poor, crippled bill would have been the death of him. As it is, he's doing fine.

Last Wednesday was St Valentine's Day when folklore says all good birds should find a mate. I noticed for the first time that day, that he was trying to carry a twig in his beak. Not very successfully because it is so contorted, but nevertheless he had got the message that this is the season for home-hunting. Because he is a bit of a cripple, he may be a little shy about popping the question, and in that case he is lucky again. Nineteen sixty-eight is Leap Year and the demurest hen black-bird can make eyes at him now, without feeling in the least immodest.

11. Watching cockney duck

March 22, 1968

I hate London. I hate all cities, but in London at this time of year the wind whistles round street corners colder, dustier and more viciously inhospitable than anywhere else I know. It is unbearably hot in summer and perishing in winter. The grumbling background of traffic and chatter of sharp Cockney voices only amplifies a stranger's loneliness.

I spent the three worst years of my life in digs in Clapham and was condemned to work in the soulless desert of Battersea. When I escaped back to my beloved Midlands, I swore that I would never set foot in London again. My work has often made me break that vow and, to my surprise, I have discovered redeeming charms, on odd-day visits, that were inscrutably hidden when I lived on the spot.

Someone told me that I should go to St James's Park to see the wild duck there, though it seemed improbable to me that any sane bird would live in such a populous spot from choice. My wife went with me and, before we got to the water's edge, it was obvious that it harboured a rich variety. We had just arrived at a vantage point when there was a shattering explosion on the opposite bank. Then another and another and another.

Smoke drifted across the water and a cloud of duck and geese and seagulls battled through it and disappeared over the horizon. The racket which had terrified the ducks infuriated us. It turned out to be one of the ceremonial occasions so beloved by Londoners. The Queen was opening Parliament and, saluting her on her way, her soldiery had blasted our hopes of bird watching with countless salvoes of cannon.

The brief glimpse of the duck we did get whetted our appetites and since then we have explored the lakes in the other London parks. In St James's Park we saw a lovely pintail drake, with feathers in his tail as long and sharp as a sergeant's waxed moustachios. His waistcoat is the sort of neat check that would enhance the most glamorous fashion model. There are pochard and tufted duck and mallard and coot and Canada geese.

It is the sort of variety at close quarters that bird watchers here in the Midlands cheerfully tramp miles to catch in the distance through powerful binoculars. Those duck on London lakes are as wild as their cousins on reservoirs here, but they behave quite differently. When they see a visitor, they swim towards him, instead of skulking as far away as possible.

We were able to walk near enough to them to distinguish the most intricate patterns of their shimmering feathers and we solved the geometry of swimming strokes that propelled them so effortlessly through the water.

Behind them, the dignified buildings of Whitehall mean no more than impassive cliffs beside the sea. They seemed to sense that the hordes of bureaucrats there, were more intent on controlling us than them.

A few of these duck will stay to breed but many will be impelled, by instinct, to foresake their easy living and return to the fastness of remote places. When they do go, they will instantly become as wild and timid as their fellows who have spent the winter in retreat from Man. Their whole personalities will change dramatically from extrovert city slickers, conning an easy living, to shy yokels who have to work for every bite and treat strangers with suspicion.

It is wonderful how adaptable wild creatures are. Many of the duck that winter on London lakes, have migrated from places where it was death to allow a man to creep within range of his gun. The cannon exploding that day temporarily shattered their complacency, for there was no way for them to know they were only loaded with blanks. They must either have supposed Cockneys to be bad marksmen or soon realised that the racket was not lethal for they were back again within an hour or so.

Yet the puny crack of a shotgun beside a country pool will depopulate it for far longer.

There is no doubt that, given a little peace, our wildlife would react in a most delightful way. I know from experience, because I have been putting the theory into practice for the last four years at Goat Lodge.

I hand-reared a few mallard, which grew up almost as tame as barnyard ducks, for the simple reason that they had never had reason to fear. Their confidence was infectious. Genuinely wild duck see ours on the pool, assume it is safe and fly down to join them. Then they waddle confidently up to the house to be fed with our own, which have never known anything else. Even very shy duck, like little teal, come as close to the window as the birds in St James's Park.

Our own duck sometimes flight round the district to neighbouring pools, where owners are keener to shoot than watch them. But away from home, they are as wary as their wild cousins. Though I have reared less than a score, there is usually a flock of around fifty feeding in the paddock.

Because I give them plenty of food, they are not tempted by hunger to take foolish risks, and the fact that the numbers do not diminish is evidence that they trust strangers less than me. The sense of security here has done wonders for other birds too. Redstarts and wagtails, grasshopper warblers and herons nest within sight of the house and the bird table is rarely without a tenant.

Their simple needs are security and food and reasonable freedom from predators. The birds in London parks prove that this co-operation is possible, even in the most densely populated places. They add beauty and movement to the most jaded city views. How much more lovely the countryside would be if wild life was not forced to flee in fear as soon as strangers showed themselves.

12. *A dose of* melophilia

March 29, 1968

I suffer from acute and incurable *melophilia*. Before you waste any sympathy on visions of psychiatric treatment or major surgery, let me reassure you that this is a rare and delightful ailment from which I am thankful I can never be healed.

I recorded about a year ago the beginning of an experiment that has since proved wholly absorbing. I bottle-reared a badger cub I saw advertised for sale. I tried very hard to get a female to rear with him because badgers are affectionate and companiable creatures. But the only one offered had been so unsuitably treated that the vet was unable to save her life. She had been dug out as a pet for children, but 'the grub didn't seem to suit her'.

This sort of treatment can cause deep misery through unimaginative ignorance. Any act that is passed for the protection of badgers should include a clause prohibiting their sale and preventing people from keeping them without a permit.

I knew that by buying my cub I probably saved him from the misery of life in a cage to which badgers are wholly unsuited. I wanted to establish him in complete liberty and observe how long it was before he reverted to the wild and ceased to be affectionate and amenable to handling.

He lived at first in an out-house with an infra-red lamp to keep him warm and he loved to romp with the dogs as soon as he was strong enough to run about. He was shut in when we couldn't watch him simply to prevent him from wandering too far and getting lost and cold away from the lamp.

Within weeks he could find his own way 'home' from anywhere in the six-acre fox-proof enclosure that includes the pool, some wood, a paddock and the house. So we fitted a rather complicated 'badger-door' consisting of two swinging flaps, and let him have the freedom of the whole enclosure.

The next step was to build him an artificial sett as he was far too small to dig one for himself. We chose a spot in an earth bank in sight of the sitting-room window. We took a great deal of trouble over this sett, making a warm, dry kennel of thick oak planks with an earthen pipe tunnel five yards long for the

41

entrance. Then we covered the whole lot with several tons of earth to insulate it and make it look natural.

It was worth all the sweat and blisters to see that young brock's delight. He shot out of sight up the tunnel as if it was his own familiar ancestral home. Then he shot out again chortling with delight to tell us of all the mod cons he'd found there. Far better, it seemed, than his ancestors had realised.

He gathered a bunch of coarse grass, held it between his chest and chin, and backed up the tunnel with it to improve the bed that had only been made by me. It was an interesting example of instinct dawning on a young animal that could not have been taught by his parents. He followed the immutable custom that badgers probably started before we had evolved from apes.

From that day to this, he has never slept anywhere else. I still put food every night in the out-house where he started. More often than not, he finds more than enough bumbling black beetles or worms or roots or juicy snails to slake his appetite and he scorns my artificial tack. Except, of course, for treacle. He adores bread and treacle, which I buy in 14 lb. tins.

When he gets up in the evening his first port of call is my study window. Not in any attempt to escape but to see if it is ajar whereupon he makes a burglarious entry to the house.

I moved his badger door to the boundary fence when he was about half-grown so that he could go through to the wood and anywhere he liked in the wide world outside. If he met any wild badgers that threatened him, all he had to do was to pop through the double doors as he'd been trained, leaving the wild badgers who would suspect a trap, thwarted outside.

Now he is a beautiful, full-grown adult badger and none could doubt his masculinity. The wild boars found him a dangerous adversary and he felt it was infra dig to be chivvied home with ignominy. So about three weeks ago he stood his ground to fight.

There was no doubt about it and plenty of evidence to prove it. Blood spots on the leaves leading to the wild badgers' sett and plenty of scars on Bill. It was flattering to find he was still affectionate and pleased to see me while he was sore, because wild animals can be dangerous to handle when they are not well.

The badgers fought it out for several nights but must have settled their territorial claims more amicably than is common with so-called civilised men. Bill now sallies forth every night into the wood. Only he and the wild badgers know the invisible frontiers they have agreed, where each must stand aside.

But we know he is still a lonely brock and were delighted to be offered last week two tiny sow cubs, their eyes only just open. They were lucky because they had been destined for execution. Soon I hope they, too, will be free to accompany Bill wherever they like. They are still very much at the baby's bottle and infra-red lamp stage – and I'm in bed with flu. So my wife is catering very capably for all of us, but I suspect at the moment she does not suffer from *melophilia* quite as acutely as I do.

The only symptom is a deep affection for badgers.

13. Death in the cornfields

April 19, 1968

Getting on for a decade ago, sportsmen and naturalists noticed foxes dying in unprecedented numbers. They are normally secretive creatures that creep quietly away to breathe their last in dignified seclusion. These foxes behaved quite out of character and left their corpses lying about stark in open fields.

Their symptoms were most distressing. At first they were dazed and hypersensitive to noise, and the terminal stages often included blindness. They were excruciatingly thirsty and their misery was so acute they even forgot to be afraid of man.

Foxes were not the only creatures that lay dying on the fair face of England. Throughout the 1950s, tens of thousands of wild birds had perished in the fields through eating insects or crops infected with the new chemical corn dressings and pesticides. The Zuckermann Working Party was formed and it examined the hazards of agricultural chemicals between 1950 to 1957 when a pesticide safety precaution scheme was set up.

The voluntary body works with a Government Advisory Committee on pesticides and other toxic chemicals to ensure safety of humans and animals and wildlife, when new pesticides are put on the market.

But during the winter of 1959/60, one thousand three hundred foxes were found dead and many more sick ones were seen. The supporters of poison for food production claimed that the foxes were dying from an obscure virus disease – but nobody could isolate the virus.

Their opponents maintained that the victims were feeding on birds which had been poisoned by eating corn dressed with Dieldrin to protect it from the wheat bulb fly. To substantiate this, they showed that the foxes and birds had pesticide residue in their tissues.

To add point to the argument, a sporting farmer fed pigeons and poultry on dressed corn and recorded the symptoms of their death, which was similar to those seen in wild birds in the cornfields of East Anglia where the plague was worst.

The dead pigeons were then fed to captive foxes, which promptly produced all the symptoms of the mysterious 'fox' disease which was also affecting badgers, dogs and cats.

The experiment attracted widespread publicity in the sporting press and succeeded in producing such a wail against poisonous pesticides from hunting and shooting men that the echoes fired public imagination.

But things still went from bad to worse and in 1960/61 no fewer than six thousand dead wild birds were counted in one place near Tumby, in Lincolnshire. The next year, over a score of different species of wild birds were picked up on the Royal estates at Sandringham, including pheasants and partridges.

Big Business acted with a great sense of responsibility, recognising the dangers of indiscriminate pest control by poison. Since 1962, manufacturers have spent about two million pounds every year on research into safer methods and less dangerous poisons. They have virtually outlawed the general use of the chlorinated hydrocarbons, including their use for sheep dip and for dressing spring-sown corn.

They have eased the catastrophic slaughter of wild life and some species, which had seemed doomed to extinction, are beginning to recover.

You might think that we should have learned our lesson from all this, but we are incurable gluttons for punishment. In 1968, forty farmers in Bedfordshire began a controlled experiment in mass slaughter. Each of them was issued with 80 lb. of tick beans, deliberately doped with *alpha chloralose* designed to stupefy wood pigeons.

Provided the birds stick to the rules, they eat just the right quantity of beans to make them stagger about like drunks. Instead of being approached by polite policemen with breath test bags, they can be gathered up by their farmer-hosts who wring their necks and bury them. It is the scientists' answer to the farmer's prayer about wood pigeons which are a pest to his crops.

Do not jump to the conclusion that Big Business is not as ethical as I made out, but wait till you can see the white in guilty eyes before you fire. The doped tick beans were not issued by commercial agricultural chemists but by the Ministry of Agriculture no less, who issued with each bag of beans a licence to spread them in the open.

This raised a nice point, because it was illegal to lay poison in the open. The Ministry claimed that this was not a poison but a narcotic. In theory, the pigeon recovers from his hangover if nobody wrings his neck.

I asked what happened if the bird did not stick to the rules but took an overdose. The Man from the Ministry agreed that it would not recover from an overdose. I feel that the difference between dying of poison and an 'overdose' of narcotic is just the sort of bureaucratic double talk of which most of us are heartily sick.

Nor is there any guarantee that only pigeons will eat the bait put down. Pheasant and partridge and wild duck can all eat whole tick beans, too. And if mice or squirrels chewed them up a bit, so could smaller birds.

Death from the pesticides of the 1950s was an accidental side-effect of insect control. I asked the Ministry man what would happen to humans if doped birds found their way to the poulterers. I had a point, he said, though they *ought* to have been buried. So I had a pipe dream about what would happen if some of those doped wood pigeons – or pheasants – found their way to the restaurant of the House of Commons. And I wondered what would be the effect of *alpha chloralose* on M.P.s' eloquence. It might make them shout as long and loud about putting poison on our land as the shooting and hunting men did.

But I doubt if they would shout so effectively.

14. Spring in the air

May 10, 1968

Now that the countryside has suddenly become so lush, it is difficult to realise how dry and starved and sterile it was before Easter. I am grateful for the built-in mechanism that shuffles such unpleasant memories under the carpet of my mind.

The east winds had been dry and 'asky' for weeks on end. We call them asky in Staffordshire when they'll give you a churchyard cough if you let them wither and dessicate you too long. I imagine it's a corruption of husky because when the cattle get a cough in summer it's always the husk as far as we're concerned.

Anyway, these asky old winds bleached the corn's rich dark greens till they were anaemic shadows of what they should have been. The buds on the trees were dry and brittle and the water in our pool a cold pneumonic grey. Nothing thrived in the garden and I gave my wife the cold comfort that a late spring is always a blessing because it limits the danger of precocious buds being nipped by late frost.

I'm no gardener and my chief concern was for the birds in the wood across the paddock. One pair of mistle thrushes had two goes at building a nest, but there was no foliage to hide it and the crows and jays took their eggs while they were still new-laid.

The herons nested according to schedule, but I didn't give much for their chances unless the weather improved, and any migratory birds that risked it seemed doomed to destruction.

Then, on Easter Tuesday, the rain came. Beautiful, warm, gentle rain that made the dry earth a drunkard. I shut my desk and wandered down the wood for the sheer luxury of watching it cleanse the foliage. Dry dust, which had clogged the bark, trickled down like soup and the buds were suddenly polished.

The corn's pallor shelled-off till you could almost see it grow, so that there was suddenly somewhere for peewits to hide their eggs and young from gormandising crows. Everything shared the sensual pleasure and a party of five fallow deer drifted out of the wood like shadows and began to guzzle the fresh-washed grass and clover in the ride.

I froze into immobility and watched them graze towards me until they were close enough for me to see the steam rising from their warm flanks and to hear the harsh rasp as they cropped the herbage. When they eventually realised I was not part of the gatepost I leaned on, the leading doe gave a snorting bark of warning and they were gone.

I'd been so absorbed that I hadn't noticed that I, too, was sopping-wet and steamy, but I was warm enough to enjoy the sensation.

Within days, the whole countryside had altered. Our wild daffodils swelled from brittle stalks with scarce a bud to maidenly, golden glory. Since then the blossom and wild flowers have been superb. Two damson trees bloomed on the edge of the wood and the wild cherries are still as virgin white as buxom brides. But it is the humble wild flowers that have given us most pleasure.

Daffodil Lawn is not a sanctuary only for wild daffs. Along the shade of the woodland boundary, there are purple patches of tiny wild violets, nestling in the shelter of the grass. There are primroses and drifts of wood anemones, or wind flowers, that shimmer in the slightest breeze more beautifully than the more extrovert daffodils. A few are a pink variant of the more common wind flower, and they blush shyly, if you examine their charms too closely.

There are ladysmocks and cowslips and the whole woodland is carpeted with bluebells. All common flowers of the English countryside. Or they all used to be.

Yet some friends of ours have just come back from Majorca where they told us they went 'specially to enjoy the wild flowers because you can't see wild flowers any more in England'. A sad commentary on modern times!

Modern farming practice is partly to blame. Hedgerows have been grubbed-out to make fields of economic size, and the wild flowers that thrived there cannot survive the sprays and fertilisers that pamper corn at the expense of every other living thing.

The rare orchids are sacrificed impartially with nettles and docks. But ours is an overcrowded island and food rightly takes priority. This overcrowding, together with affluence, spills more people, with more leisure, out onto the countryside than ever before. Although they have mastered the complicated techniques of modern living, many of them seem incapable of assimilating the simple fact that, if they pick wild flowers, instead of leaving them to seed, there will be fewer to pick next year.

So a Bill for the Protection of Wild Flowers was put before Parliament to make it an offence to pick the most threatened species. The damage done by us, the public, will be minimised and a few more wild flowers will survive.

But, to be effective, the Bill must control the activities of the bureaucrats too. Roadside verges are among the very few places where wild flowers could not only thrive but be enjoyed by the maximum number of people.

Officialdom is tidy-minded. At this moment, local authorities are busily spraying verges with weed-killer to kill the 'weeds' and with growth-inhibitor (horrible jargon word!) to slow down recovery even of the wizened grass.

If all the crowd from the Cup Final picked wild flowers for forty hours a week they couldn't match the efficient devastation of one tractor creeping inexorably along the lane with weed-killer. Our legislators take infinite care to curtail the public's activities but bury their heads in the mud when official sprayers pass by.

15. Dove dirge

May 17, 1968

For almost a fortnight we have been hearing strange noises in our wood; a continuous, repetitive mumbo-jumbo of meaningless sound. It is a foreign tongue, mouthing a complaint about English weather and the uncharitable habits of English natives.

We had an influx of these visitors a couple of years ago and again last year, but conditions didn't suit them and they pushed-off or perished. I never discovered which.

The latest wave seem tougher and quite determined to consolidate their position. 'Wave' is perhaps an exaggeration because so far there are only two. But the row they kick up would not disgrace a primitive orchestra. Although their song is such a bore, they are most comely birds to look at. Their most distinguishing feature is a smart black collar, open at the throat, and they wear a delightful creamy-bluff mantle. They are close relations of my favourite summer visitors, the turtle doves, which do not have the same black collar, but are endowed with spotted mantles of a beautiful, delicate chestnut shade.

Fine feathers may make fine birds but it is all too easy for them to put you off the moment they open their beaks. That is the failing of collared doves, the birds that have invaded our woods. Turtle doves have a wonderfully seductive, crooning song, which succeeds in making English woodlands the most charming spot on earth. But their wretched cousins yak on as endlessly as nagging women.

You may have guessed by now that I am not overjoyed about the visit of our uninvited guests, but I do try to act like a civilised host and disguise my lack of enthusiasm.

In these days when many of us are engaged in a continual battle to save threatened species from extinction, it is at least a refreshing change to find a creature that can hold its own and is actually extending its range, as collared doves are doing. Up to the last war, they were rare visitors to these shores and bird watchers got very excited if they saw one. Then, for some unknown reason, their population increased dramatically and they spread rapidly north west over Europe, and came over here in numbers first as summer migrants.

They bred rapidly and some of them stayed as full-blown immigrants and they are now gradually colonising the country. Several came to our wood a couple of years ago and at first we were delighted to see them and sad when they soon disappeared. I never quite made up my mind whether they travelled further on or if they were killed by owls or other predators.

They tried again last year and stayed long enough for me to realise just how monotonous their perpetual row could be. I felt like giving the local owls the tip-off that free dinners were available. But the wood soon reverted to its normal peace without any sinister help from me.

Now they have come again and they show every sign of integrating permanently, so we natives will just have to put up with them. I am only sorry that it could not have been their cousins, the Barbary doves, who decided to come.

Barbary doves are smaller, and their colour is a more delicate cream with a voice as attractive as the most dulcet turtle dove. They have an endearing quality of being almost suicidally tame and confiding, with a most affectionate streak. When we were at our last house, I bought a pair of Barbary doves, which are quite cheap, and commonly kept in aviaries.

I made a temporary cage at a loft window, where they could sit and look out at their surrounding but retreat into the loft for protection against cold and predators. I hate keeping birds in cages, but hoped, as soon as they were settled, that I could remove the cage so that they could fly free by day, but return to the safety of the loft at dusk.

It worked like a charm. For a few nights I did have to pop them back into the loft, but they were so tame that they allowed me to pick them up as easily as if I had reared them by hand. They soon made a nest and reared two young – and then I got a shock.

These little Barbary doves were far prettier and more delicate than the collared doves that have just come to live with us. Their voices were so gently persuasive that it was impossible to visualise them doing an unkind deed. Yet, as soon as their young were reared, the affection withered in the old birds' breasts and they drove them out ruthlessly into the world from the safety of the loft. Within nights, the inevitable had happened and the owls had eaten them.

But the original pair prospered and we grew very fond of them in spite of their fickle affections. They were inordinately keen on food and when I fed the poultry they flew down into the open corn bins and guzzled the wheat as soon as I opened the lids.

I was naturally very careful to turn them out before I closed the bins, but the corn merchant arrived with fresh supplies when I was out, and he knew nothing about our Barbary doves' foibles. He opened the lid, returned to his lorry for a bag of wheat – and emptied it into the bin. While he was away, the doves had flown into the bottom of the bin to feed – and I never discovered what had happened to them till the bin was almost empty again.

'Our' new collared doves, which have arrived of their own accord, show every sign of growing just as tame and greedy. But, however plaintively they plead, I shall never allow them to learn what delights and what dangers lie at the bottom of our corn bin.

16. Holiday at home

May 31, 1968

I never visit the seaside, if I can help it, because I hate all crowds of more than two or three and it becomes harder every year to find the deserted beaches of my childhood. But the real reason for my horror of the sea is that its ceaseless turgid roar evokes uneasy visions in my subconscious mind.

A nagging voice inside me insists that the rocks, now silhouetted in dramatic individuality, are doomed to be ground to anonymous dust. Gales blow the tragedy of shipwrecked sailors inland and the softest breeze whispers of loneliness when close friends sail away. Even the therapy of ogling the girls palls, in time. Their swimsuits are so scanty that it becomes apparent that they are really as stereotyped as the identical grains of sand they lie on.

So I spend my holidays at home and fill my mind with simpler things. I derive satisfaction from making small clearings in the wood, where animals can feed in view, or carving woodland rides in spacious curves. A tree grubbed out may open a gap to the skyline that will give a pleasant vista from the house or reveal a view to rolling, unspoilt countryside.

It is a pastime that must not be pursued in haste, because it is all too easy to remove the wrong branch or sapling that would take years of growth to replace.

There were five old hawthorn trees, to the south of the house, that obscured the hills of Cannock Chase, ten miles or so away. We thought that, instead of allowing these trees to shut the paddock in, we would take them out for the sake of the view it would give.

The one snag was that, six miles away, the great cooling towers of Rugeley Power Station huddled in the valley. This was a squalid prospect we could do without but precise surveying revealed that it would be safe to take out four of the trees if we left the fifth to blot out the power station.

One of the joys of a holiday is that the unwonted exercise creates an enormous appetite for food and drink which is followed by repleted drowsiness.

Our four great hawthorns were thirty feet or so in height,

with butts as fat as drunkards' bellies. Thorn is a tough, hard wood, and felling hawthorns an exercise to tax the muscles of a weight-lifter. The project began by rousing the primitive vandal urge which revels in sheer destruction but we found that nothing would cure the disease of vandalism so surely as prolonged hard labour.

Before the second tree was down, the exhilaration had been deflated by work and the only incentive was the artist's creative urge which strives to paint a view upon the canvas. The masterpiece we were conceiving, would be a living picture of everchanging colour and stereoscopic depth, shifting with sun and rain at dawn and dusk.

The third tree convinced us that all labour was mean and hard labour meanest of all. The most heavenly view could not possibly be worth the sweat and aches of this, and it was only the masochistic dedication of monks in Lent that drove us to start to fell the last great tree. This was bigger than all the others and as hard as iron. The boughs were thicker than the trunks of normal trees and even the smallest twigs had thorns like bayonets.

At last it creaked and crashed in homage to the biting blade. The skyline suddenly opened round the solitary survivor and, to the right were Hednesford hills, veiled in green pine woods, to which distance lent a soft, protective haze. The dreaded cooling towers and belching chimney stacks are obliterated by the last thorn, blossoming at the moment in white flowers to celebrate that it alone survived.

So we retired to admire the results of our labours through a pair of binoculars. It was astonishing what the removal of four hawthorns had done and we felt our aches and pains a small price to pay.

But holidays at home can be relaxing as well as energetic and mine provide plenty of opportunities for watching bathing beauties as beautiful and far more varied than any at the sea. My bathing beauties perform their ablutions in shallow water, and I was introduced to the best way to watch them by my friend Stanley Porter.

He spends most of his holidays in more gentle pursuits than hacking down trees. He takes a comfortable seat in concealment and watches the birds in their baths. Nor is he content only to watch. At critical moments, he squeezes the trigger of his camera and preserves their beauty for posterity.

I trust that he will forgive me for revealing some of the

secrets of his photographic art, but I have found his methods just as useful to folks like me, who are content only to stand and stare. He saunters quietly around till he finds a secluded puddle and in dry weather he will even bestir himself so far as to make one artificially and fill it by the bucketful. A less energetic form of landscape gardening than ours, but effective on a smaller scale.

Then he disappears into his photographic hide, anoints himself with oil to repel the midges, and settles down to watch. To take a portrait of a bird bathing, for example, he has to work at close quarters and, within half a day, fifteen species had been to bathe in convenient focus, as much for his pleasure as for theirs.

The bath they chose was the hearthrug-sized puddle he had landscaped with his trowel, instead of with the labouring gangs of Capability Brown. It would be difficult to capture such beauty with less effort than that.

17. Seven for a secret?

June 7, 1968

My generation was reared in hard times and scratched by edges rough enough to start a revolution nowadays. Opposite the house where I was born in Bloxwich, there was still a group of old farm buildings. They were symbolic of the rural mentality that survived in the Black Country long after the industrial haze had stifled green crops and clanking trams had drowned the song of birds.

We always referred to 'the village' and most of us had fathers or grandfathers born in deep country, who had bred in us an instinctive nostalgia for country things.

Times were hard enough for hard-worked men to start again at the end of a long day to work for themselves instead of for a master. After tea, they cultivated their allotments for the simple reason that their money didn't stretch to the luxury of buying vegetables from shops.

Their wives usually kept a pig in a sty in the yard, because 'you could eat all of a pig, but his squeal', and it was not only the cheapest meat they could buy, but the sweetest too.

Even as a child, I marvelled at the fickleness of these warm-hearted women. For six months, they cossetted their pigs as pampered pets, calling them by name and grooming their coats with a dandy brush. But when the time came to convert them to bacon, they turned out, with glee, to watch the local pig-sticker ply his gory trade, without so much as a crocodile tear.

Country folk still have the same primitive outlook. They are fond of animals and take great pride in growing them well, in good conditions, to reach their prime in the bloom of health. But, when their crop is ripe, be it a field of corn, a forest of trees, or a litter of pigs, it is harvested with the same lack of sentiment.

Such a practical outlook is a strange bed-fellow for the country superstitions that still stalk in the dusk down every country lane.

Yet tough chaps still doff their caps in mock servility if a single magpie crosses their path, and their wives still mumble the time-worn jingle:

One for sorrow, two for joy,
Three for a girl, four for a boy,
Five for silver, six for gold,
Seven for a secret, never to be told.

It isn't only magpies that stir unimaginative country hearts. If tragedy upon tragedy piles on some apparently innocent head, the answer is always simple. He may not have noticed it at the time, but the victim has probably killed a robin, or

Nightjars and ravens, with wide stretched throats,
From yews and hollies send their baleful notes.

Country folk still place more faith in the birds than the Met. Office:

If the robin sings in the bush,
The weather will be coarse.
If he sings in the barn,
The weather will be warm.

It's all rather clever, because there is always a contradictory superstition and, by quoting the right one, you can never be wrong.

There is an old shed, at the top of our wood, where the Bagot goats shelter in the winter. I often slip up there, to watch from the gloom, the creatures in the wood outside.

This year the bird song has been superb: an absolute chorus of robins 'singing in the barn'. By that portent, the weather should be warm. But, in the corner of the shed, a blackbird built her nest, reared a brood of young, and is now sitting on a second clutch of eggs. Country folk will tell you that blackbirds do not build inside unless there is going to be a bad summer. 'A sure sign' they say 'of bad weather to come'. You can't go wrong, can you – unless you quote the wrong superstition.

The cuckoo is always regarded as the harbinger of spring. Opinions about what is a 'good' spring may vary but this year, the late, wet season and absence of frosts have certainly blessed us with a superb crop of all sorts of blossom, from hawthorn to fruit trees.

Perhaps it is no coincidence that I have heard more cuckoos call than I can remember for years. It is certainly no coincidence that cuckoos are also associated with fertility and fidelity in marriage. They have all the fun of courtship but none of the responsibilities. They deposit their eggs in the nest of unsuspecting birds, which they leave to have all the trouble of rearing the young cuckoos, while they fly on and philander again.

Watching any sort of courtship has always been a traditional rural sport, and practical country folk have naturally drawn parallels between cuckoos and their neighbours. A husband, whose wife is unfaithful, has been cuckolded. And maidens count the number of times the cuckoo calls for the first time in the season, to predict how many children they'll have or how many years it will be before they marry. In some parts, before they married, it was customary to catch a young cuckoo and put him in a cage as a talisman to ensure fertility.

Although country folk are often so observant, it is astonishing what gaps there are in their knowledge.

The cuckoo comes in April,
He sings his song in May,
Then in June, he'll change his tune,
And in July, he'll fly away.

Well, 'he' doesn't change his tune, except for the hoarse hiccuping, supposed to be caused by an egg sticking in his throat. The change in tune is the lovely liquid, bubbling mating cry of the female.

But the first prize for cuckoo lore should be awarded to the ancient writer Pliny, who said that if you collected the earth round your right foot when you heard the first cuckoo, it would be the perfect flea repellent. I tried it last year, and I haven't had a single flea since.

18. Thunder in the wood

July 12, 1968

The thick mat of grass, in the shade of the wood, was warm as a clammy hand. The only sound was the persistent drone of millions of flies. They were high in the canopy of trees and posed no more threat than bombers set on course for far-off places.

But the air was almost tangible with humidity and hot enough to make it too much effort even to lounge in comfort. To the south, over Cannock Chase, black clouds were massing in promise of blessed rain to cool and clear the air. From where I sat, I could look right across the vale and watch the birth-pangs of the storm.

The first symptom was a belching rumble so deep and subdued that the vibration was communicated more by feeling than sound. It might have passed unnoticed if it had not set up a chorus of crowing by every cock pheasant in the wood. They kick up the same row at the sound of distant explosions, but skulk in sensible silence at the more immediate danger of the crack of sporting guns.

As soon as I heard them crow, I knew that any rain that came would be introduced by thunderous orchestrations. My suspicions were confirmed when leaves on the topmost branches above me began to flutter and dance for no apparent reason. At ground level there was not a breath of moving air and all was still as the peace before the storm. As soon as I heard the whispered warning of the leaves, I goaded myself to movement and shifted out into the open.

I'm not in the least superstitious about thunder and neither turn our mirrors to the wall nor cover the fire-irons with the hearthrug. And I just do not believe that a steel knife will add appreciably to the impending risk of doom; nor that lightning never strikes in the same place twice – because I know quite well it does.

A famous landmark in Bagot's Park, behind our house, is a solitary oak called Lord Bagot's Walking Stick. He would have been a tall Lord Bagot who used it as such, because the naked trunk is 75 feet high before it sprouts a branch. There is a curving scar down the bark where lightning played in 1903, and last year three separate strikes used it again as a conductor. It convinces me that there is no safe shelter beneath any tree, whether it has been struck before or not.

Seconds after I moved out of the wood, the warm blanket of damp air at ground level was folded up before the storm. There was one puff of steamy breath, followed by the luxury of a sweet, cool breeze. It came in such an unexpected gust that the tree tops flexed and cowered as if they feared the lightning would soon choose them as victims.

The subdued distant rumblings rolled closer and louder while huge crocodile tears of rain lamented the damage before it was done. The shroud of cloud over the Chase drifted slowly in our direction and as it came, jagged forks of lightning stabbed impartially down.

Nothing can cut you to size more surely than the contemplation of such a storm. Its retribution is a random selection, as likely to hit a church tower as an ugly factory stack. Saints and sinners share the same chances of survival.

The great cooling towers of Rugeley power station reared stark between the storm and me. They were symbolic of Man's conquest of the elements and had harnessed electricity to be our slave. I speculated on the irony of fate if electric power beyond Man's making should strike them down.

The grey curtain of rain was a heavy veil to soften the details of destruction, making things seem better than they were. A butterfly which had been sunning itself until the clouds gathered, crawled under a bracken frond for shelter. A transient delusion of security.

A few yards from where I sat, a hen pheasant called her chicks to the stump of an old tree, which sprouted again in defiance of the woodman's axe. She treated the first rain drops as a luxury, spreading her wings and fluffing out her feathers for the sensual pleasure of cleansing them of dust. Her chicks, not much bigger than sparrows, were still downy and cheeped their complaints that they were getting waterlogged. The old bird shuffled right under the butt of the tree and spread her wings, as Nature's first umbrella, for the whole brood to creep close to her for warmth.

Thunderstorms, at this time of year, wreak immeasurable havoc especially with young pheasants and partridges. An old country saying claims that more partridges are hatched on mid-summer day than all the days in the year. If there are bad thunderstorms in the next few weeks, lots of young birds are too weak to force their way through dripping grass and perish by the wayside. The stronger ones get sodden and often die from pneumonia.

My mind was taken off the plight of birds by the mounting fury of the storm. The cracks were so sharp that they sizzled almost simultaneously with the flash. Most people, I suppose, would have gone home, but thunder holds a primitive fascination for me. It pierces the gloss of civilisation and emphasises how puny are the works of Man. Our ancestors worshipped Thor, the God of Thunder, who will still roar with ribald mirth when we are dust.

When the storm was over, I wandered round to see what had flinched before its power. One tree, in particular, burnt its image on my mind. It was an ash, on the road to Rugeley, and lightning had peeled its rough bark as easily as a child would skin a twig. A curving crack was riven right through its trunk, and though the leaves at the top are not yet withered, the remains stand white and gaunt as the bones in a sepulchre.

It is a very humbling sight.

19. The other side of the fence

July 26, 1968

A letter in my postbag about a month ago was very close to my heart. It came from a farmer's wife, near Wokingham, who was in trouble with her goose. It was a wild goose that had arrived out of the blue as a tiny gosling one or two days old. Pond Wood is on the edge of their farm and Canada geese sometimes nest there.

Perhaps this tiny gosling had been orphaned or had dropped out of the convoy when its mother was moving her brood from the nest there to safer quarters.

It was wise to choose Mrs Chandler as hostess for she has a very soft heart. She kept her visitor in a warm box by night, and a chicken run by day, with short, sweet grass to graze and bread-and-milk for afters.

All went well for a month, and the gosling and its mistress wove a powerful web of mutual affection. The first snag was that, although they are normally such sociable birds, the farm geese made no secret of their resentment and seemed quite determined to kill the foundling the moment they could get at it.

A less immediate threat was human. Young thugs in the district round the farm scoured the countryside with guns and stones, amusing themselves by persecuting anything that moved.

So Mrs Chandler decided that her gosling must go, and go soon; it must have time to adopt its new quarters as home before it was old enough to fly away to danger. She had heard about our sanctuary and wrote to ask if Wee, as she called her gosling, could join the other creatures here.

Now Canada geese, when they are adult, can be pretty aggressive and are not really the best neighbours for the smaller varieties of ornamental waterfowl. People who keep choice collections of birds look down on anything as common as Canadas.

We are not so snooty and our pool is plenty large enough for the weaker to find security. We even got excited this spring when a pair of wild Canada geese, which were obviously house hunting for a nesting site, put us on their short-list. They stayed with us for about a month, coming right up to the house to feed with the ducks, but eventually decided to settle elsewhere.

We thought that the gosling from Wokingham might mate with one of their flock next spring, so I replied to Mrs Chandler that her gosling would be very welcome to try its luck here. We expected it to arrive by rail, but its mistress was far too fond of it to risk such uncertainty and discomfort. She and her husband brought it all the way by car.

I was not surprised to find that it had a pronounced human fixation. One of the snags of rearing very young animals and birds is that they may regard the human who tends them as their own mother. They may acquire a fixation for human beings every bit as difficult to conquer as the fixations that humans acquire for drugs.

Geese are exceptionally susceptible to these fixations and the controlling factor often seems to be the first moving object they see after hatching. This is normally the mother goose that hatched the eggs, but cases have been recorded of geese becoming attached to cattle and sheep and even to inanimate objects like wheelbarrows.

Mrs Chandler's Canada goose was 'fixed' on humans and, as soon as it was left, it set-up the plaintive, high pitched wails that had given it the name of Wee.

It seemed far too small to risk loose on the pool, because it was not fully feathered and its down might have become so waterlogged that it could contract pneumonia. So I put it in a wire netting chicken run on the grass beside the house where we could keep an eye on it.

Its run at home had been surrounded by corrugated iron sheets so that it could not see if the grass was greener on the other side of the fence. With this restricted view, captivity must have seemed so inevitable that other ideas never occurred to it. It had never seen wire netting and when it landed in our run, it could not believe that anything looking so fragile was really strong enough to imprison it.

It started to pace up and down crying pitifully and rubbing its bill on the rough netting until the horny surface began to scale. It was so miserable that I let it out into the greater area of the yard and paddock where the dogs run when they are not in the house with us. It immediately strode to the nearest boundary netting and continued its frustrated pacing interminably as a tiger in a cage. It only stopped when we went out, when its overwhelming yearning for human company temporarily conquered all other urges.

It followed like a shadow every pace we took, but as soon as it was left alone it resumed its subconscious reflex pacing up and down the nearest wire netting. Most stupid of all, whenever I put it on the other side of the netting to see where it wanted to go, it simply paced up and down to try to get back again.

My only consolation was that its mistress was far away, in blissful ignorance of how restless the poor creature was. I feared that the fixation was incurable and that it was destined to spend most of its life vainly fretting to be near to people.

Then we had a piece of luck. The damage from rubbing against the netting could only be avoided by persuading it to keep away from the boundary, so I chose the risk of getting it waterlogged on the pool as a lesser evil.

The moment it touched the wider water there was a complete transformation. Its confiding, affectionate domesticity shelled off and it instantly became wilder than the wildest wild duck. It couldn't yet fly but instinct showed that its safest refuge was the very centre of the pool. It came to the bank to graze, but it no longer wanted bread-and-milk.

Nor has it shown the slightest interest in human beings. It has transferred its affection to the Bewicks swan, which has been here since it flew into an electric wire and broke a wing eighteen months ago. The swan is now tame and comes to the house for corn, so his friend the goose comes with him. They are inseparable and the goose is a wild goose once more, and I am truly thankful as much for our peace of mind as for the bird's.

20. The Queen works herself to death

September 13, 1968

The ripe plums in the shops this week are sweet with tender temptation that no wasp can resist. A mild winter and moist spring have made this a year to remember for bounteous fruit.

The borders of our wood are scarlet with mountain ash and honeysuckle berries, and our young Victoria plum at last has overcome her shyness. Shedding her inhibitions, she has produced so many young plums that I have had to ease the burden by supporting her branches with props.

When I noticed the swarms of wasps in the local town it dawned on me how few there were out here. Most years they are a pest, because they find the shelter of the wood and its variety of food exactly to their liking.

For several years I have found a score of hollows where the wild badgers have scooped out their nests. They love to feast on the succulent grubs which would otherwise have grown into a menacing chorus of wasps. So I assumed, at first, that the plague of wasps in the town might be related to the fact that no badgers roam in its gardens.

The theory doesn't hold water. The close-flowering heads of red sedum by the sitting-room window have been weighed down with innumerable bumble bees for a week or more, and the sweet honey in the bumble bees' nests is among the badgers' favourite food. So, if it were the badgers we have to thank for keeping our plum tree free of wasps, it is reasonable to assume they would have cleared the bumble bees as well.

I am glad they didn't because the two dozen or so different species of bumble bees which live in Britain are among my favourite insects. I have the utmost respect for them, despite the fact that they are such a matriarchal society.

Every nest has, as its directing force, a queen bee. She leaves the nest about this time of year and spends her one romantic moment on her brief honeymoon with the first mate that succeeds in capturing her. Then she finds what she hopes will prove a suitable spot to lie dormant for the winter. She buries herself under the dead leaves of a hedgerow or in the roots of a tussock of grass, but her chances of survival are pretty slim.

If the bank faces south, a flashy spell of wintry sun may tempt her out too soon so that she perishes in the first cold night which follows. A dry spot may flood in melting snow; a shrew may hunt and devour her, or she may fall prey to parasitic worms.

But some do survive despite the odds and emerge in the first fickle warmth of spring. The early days are a grim battle for sheer survival, and the young queen has to expend every mite of her energy simply going from flower to flower collecting enough pollen and nectar to maintain a spark of life.

Then, as spring flowers grow more plentiful, the surplus food brings her into breeding condition. A subconscious urge to found a family drives her to go house-hunting with such dedication that she will fight a rival queen to the death for a coveted site. This may be a field mouse's discarded nest or a tunnel under a tussock of grass.

When she has moved in, she produces wax from between the segments of her belly and fashions her first cell. She fills this with pollen and eats the surplus. This high protein diet soon stimulates her to lay her first batch of eggs, on top of the pollen inside the cell, and she covers them with another sheet of wax.

Then she builds a waxen honey pot which she fills as a reserve to feed the brood that will hatch from the eggs on the pollen. Besides collecting enough food for herself and her young, she nurtures the brood like a broody hen, lying across them with her body to raise their temperature and accelerate their development. If conditions get warmer or more humid than she wants, she creates a current of air with her wings to bring the temperature down again and ventilate the nest.

The eggs hatch into grubs, which turn into cocoons and eventually emerge as adult bees. Their devoted mother even acts as midwife and bites a hole in their cocoon to help them out. None of the early youngsters will grow up to be queens. They will be under-sexed females, fitted only to be workers. Mere humble bees. They start at once to take over the duties of collecting pollen and nectar for the whole community so that the queen can concentrate on producing eggs.

She is no mere mechanical production belt because she has a marvellous built-in mechanism for family planning. The number of eggs she lays is not haphazard either. They are not even simply proportional to the number of workers available to feed them. This family planning is so sophisticated that it actually forecasts the number of eggs and larvae which will have emerged as workers by the time the latest batch of eggs hatch out. This process goes on all summer and builds up as large and thriving a colony as possible. When autumn comes, the queen will be worn out by her labours and die. So will her workers.

Continuity is assured by the queen suddenly producing young sexually mature queens and male drones, whose task in life is to make love but never work. The cycle is complete. This is the link between the past and the future and the young mated queens seek sanctuary for the winter.

21. *Disease spread by fleas and man*

September 27, 1968

Looking out of the window, at first light the other morning, I was surprised to see a baby rabbit on the lawn. So far as I know, there is not even one small colony of wild rabbits nearer than a mile from us and this tiny creature had neither the physique nor the maturity to make a likely miler.

Our garden is in the same enclosure as the paddock, the pool and part of the wood where we keep ducks and golden pheasants safe from foxes, with a wire-netting fence. This is six feet high and its base is buried in the ground. Each mesh is only two inches across which is too small for any but the youngest rabbit to creep through.

So the origin of our visitor is wrapped in mystery. I do not know where he came from and, if he did squeeze through the netting, it must have been some time ago, because he is obviously too big now to squeeze back.

The Ministry of Agriculture is always telling us what pests rabbits are and that they must be exterminated ruthlessly, to the last one. So duty calls me to shoot him. Whatever the Ministry says about the dangerously explosive breeding habits of rabbits, ours can't get out to find a mate and he can't increase his species by himself.

So I shall probably continue to observe this rabbit, which has sentenced himself to solitary confinement, through Nelson's unseeing eye; and I should be tempted to conceal his whereabouts from Authority in a positive smokescreen of white lies.

A wild rabbit first took my eye at the age of four or five. I had gone to a local estate with my father, who was doctor to the squire and his family. Left by myself in the car by the front door, I noticed a whole colony of rabbits of all ages and sizes, grazing on the lawns which crept up to the rolling parkland beyond.

Watching, enthralled, I coveted one as a pet and when my father returned I begged him to ask the squire if he would give me one. The old man overheard my request and said: 'Next time you come, my lad, bring some salt to put on their tails and you can have all you can catch.'

I thought, then, that he was the most wonderfully generous man I'd ever met – but I soon grew older and wiser. I learned as a schoolboy that salt on their tails was no substitute for a good ferret and a pocketful of silent purse nets.

Gradually, my hand increased its cunning until, by the time I had left school, I knew the poacher's art better than the more respectable subjects on my curriculum.

Although I have caught more than my share of rabbits since, I have always had a sneaking regard for them. I could never understand those who thought that financial gain justified the use of steel gin traps, which held them by their shattered legs until the trapper made his round again. And the very thought of deliberate inoculation with myxomatosis to exterminate them is too horrible to contemplate. It is the most obscene disease misused by man.

The deliberate spreading of disease and the use of gin traps have been made illegal now. And so they should. But there is still said to be a black market in diseased rabbits to spread the plague among their healthy fellows, so I am rather on the rabbits' side – as I am with almost any threatened species.

I admire his tenacity of life and, above all, I admire his adaptability. My childhood rabbits, in the squire's park, lived in burrows and came into the open only to feed when they bit off the acid sward as close as a bowling green so that there was not a blade of cover to conceal or shelter them.

Their teeming numbers so overcrowded their warrens that the least whiff of disease spread through them like a spark through tinder. This congestion was perfect for myxomatosis which can spread only by inoculation. It is normally transmitted when a rabbit flea bites an unaffected rabbit after feeding on tainted blood.

The first waves of the disease wiped out almost one hundred per cent of its victims. There were not enough survivors to graze the herbage close and, for the first time in years, there was enough natural regeneration of the vegetation to provide dense cover. This is exactly what rabbits like. They choose a warren only as a retreat from predators or in bad weather, so that the survivors forsook their burrows for cosy 'sits' in rushes or briars.

This gave them less contact with other rabbits, so that they were not so likely to be bitten by a flea that had fed on a victim. This change of habit, from living underground to becoming a 'bush rabbit', living on the surface, is not a conscious and intelligent way of avoiding the plague, although it is just as effective. It is a natural acceptance of more pleasant conditions created by the flush of denser vegetation.

Our little rabbit on the lawn seems to have gone one better still. He has chosen ground unfouled by rabbits for several years and makes cosy 'sits' in the shrubbery or in my wife's cherished clumps of flowers.

She has a soft heart though and he is safe from her. All that is necessary to fill his cup of joy is for another little rabbit to creep through the netting and stay till she is too big to get back again.

22. The death knell of the hunt?

October 4, 1968

The fox hunting season is with us again, but I do not propose to become involved in the emotional arguments that often engulf it. Whatever the ethical theories may be, I wish to examine the plain practicalities which I believe will influence the future of hunting.

Fox hunting is not the traditional sport some would have us believe. Nor is it so ancient. Until the eighteenth century, the countryside was far more heavily wooded than it is now, and less densely populated. The clearings for farming were mainly confined to the surroundings of scattered towns and villages.

This type of terrain was suitable for hunting hares, which tend to keep to their own relatively small territory and, therefore, to run in circles on the open farmland. It was not really suitable for foxes, which simply disappeared into deep woodland where horsemen could not follow.

As the population grew, and more and more land was enclosed for farming, there was enough suitable hunting country to give foxes the doubtful honour of promotion from 'vermin' to 'respectable sporting quarry'.

So it was about two centuries ago when many harrier packs changed their quarry from hares to foxes and became foxhounds. The real heyday of fox hunting was between one and two centuries ago. Vast estates, in single ownership, were farmed by tenant farmers.

Many landowners placed such store by their sport that they would dispossess a farmer if he killed so much as a pheasant on his land, and they were in the position to give the hunt permission to go wherever they wanted on the estate, however much hardship it caused. Any farmer who objected had a simple alternative. He could get out.

Resentment at having a hundred horsemen galloping over growing crops was so sharp that it drove a wedge between tenant farmers and hunting landlords which many predicted would finish hunting – if many people ever owned the land they farmed.

That was a period of privilege and the damage hunting did

to those living in the countryside was not confined to the arrogant trampling of growing crops. Poultry, in those days, really was kept on free range. Farmyard fowls could wander where they liked and were expected to get much of their own living gleaning on the stubbles and beating the sparrows to odd grains of corn spilt in the rickyard.

They were easy prey for Charlie Fox, who was immune from retribution. 'Vulpicide' – killing a fox by unconventional methods – was considered by many to be at least a social crime. Even wealthy shooting men could find themselves ostracised in the country if a fox was included in their bag or their keepers were caught killing one.

Times have changed since then. Many estates have been broken up by death duties and many farmers have bought the land their ancestors tilled as tenants. They are now in a position to forbid the hunt to cross their land and to claim damages for any harm they do.

Add to this the fact that the Forestry Commission has been planting marginal land with trees since the 1920s, so that there are vast tracts of unhuntable forest again as there were before fox hunting began.

The odds against hunting are obviously mounting. At the same time, some changing factors have acted the other way because recent variations to farming methods have minimised potential damage in some respects. More poultry is now kept shut in deep litter houses or battery cages, where they are immune from predation by foxes and never call on hunt 'poultry funds'. Cattle are 'yarded' in winter, so that there is less chance of them being stampeded through hedges.

To cap it all, a more prosperous agriculture has bestowed more leisure and more cash on the farming community. So, instead of farmers forbidding the hunt to cross their land as was predicted, many of them have jumped on the wagon and hunt and shoot as avidly as their landlords did before them.

But, the very prosperity that made this possible, has produced complications. Growing mechanisation needs larger fields for the giant machines to manoeuvre. And the most enthusiastic hunting farmer is scarcely likely to welcome an army of horsemen, advancing across his rich prairie. Most important of all, this corn may well be surrounded by a barbed wire fence and may even be near to a motorway.

The more affluent hunts can cope with barbed wire fences by paying for post-and-rail jumping gaps. But money won't buy the right to allow hounds or horsemen on motorways. More traffic on the roads, more roads and railways forbidden to loose hounds, more barbed wire and larger fields are the writing on the wall.

Shooting men rent the sporting rights before a shot is fired, while hunting men do not. They cannot, because they do not know the way the fox will lead the hounds. This sometimes engenders more friction between hunting and shooting men than between farmers and either.

There may be more people with horses than at any time since the motor car clattered into our lives, and possibly more numerical support for hunting. But however keen the support may be, I believe that sheer physical pressure of land usage will sound the death knell of fox hunting, whether we like it or will be glad to see it gone.

23. This goddess weaves eternally

October 25, 1968

Far be it from me to defend the macabre customs of spiders. I know perfectly well that many of them capture their victims by unsporting stealth. I know that spider wives may devour their husbands and become, in turn, satisfying meals for their own offspring.

Some foreign species are poisonous and I was brought up on terrifying tales at my mother's knee. She used to describe midnight tropical safaris, with slippers as weapons. Her quarry was a giant tarantula spider, as big as a plate, which had invaded the privacy of her bedroom. I listened spell-bound, eager for the gory climax of the hunt. Then I crept terrified to bed, fearful lest nightmares should inflate her victim to man-eating proportions.

Despite that, I am very fond of spiders. My mother understood my childish thirst for spine-chilling horror stories, and she knew that I enjoyed the pretence of being frightened by her tarantula.

I am fond of spiders because I admire the shining symmetry of autumn spiders' webs; I envy them their craftsmanship and I praise their overwhelming zeal for work.

At this time of year, when mornings are chilly, I love to be out early after a touch of frost. Hedgerows and bracken, mellowed gold by autumn tints, are festooned with most delicate jewellery. Minute beads of frost pick out the tracery of every fragile thread so that the intricate geometry is lined in scintillating gossamer.

These webs are obvious to the most unobservant, not so much because there are more than usual at this time of the year. It is because heavy dews and rimey frosts emphasise their artistry.

The mechanism of spinning such webs is a minor miracle in itself. A spider has a battery of highly complicated spinnerets, with which she spins her web. They look rather like fingers and one ancient writer said that a spider 'hath fingers that the most gallant virgins desire to have theirs like them, long, slender, round and of exact feeling. And her skin is so soft, smooth

74

polished and neat that she precedes the softest skinn'd mayds and the daintiest and most beautiful strumpets.'

Although we might not rate strumpets less attractive than the daintiest spider, there is no doubt that spiders' spinnerets are unsurpassed at weaving. Our most brilliant engineers have not invented a process to produce a thread so fine, so perfect, so strong.

Before they contradict me and begin to boast, let me warn them what once happened in ancient Greece. The goddess Athene believed that nobody could approach her prowess at weaving and, when Arachne challenged her supremacy, she turned her into a spider and doomed her to weave until eternity.

So every spider you see is descended from Arachne and that is why spiders are not insects but *Arachnidae*. There are other distinctions from insects, too. Insects have three pairs of legs, but spiders four. And text books say the spiders have 'simple' eyes, though they may have six pairs or so. Insects, on the other hand, have 'compound' eyes, which have thousands of facets, like jewellers cut on diamonds, to make them reflect the light.

Each facet in an insect's eye is connected by a tiny tube to the retina. This does not focus an image like a human eye, but transmits a spot of light, brighter or darker than the spots around. The general effect is to produce a jumble of spots which form a pattern, like a picture in a newspaper.

If you think it a tall story that spiders are not insects, but descendants of Arachne, watch the miracle of a garden spider spinning her web. She exudes a bead of moisture from her spinneret, which turns to pure silk when exposed to air. This thread floats gently off in the wind until it attached itself to the first solid object it touches. The spider pulls it tight and uses it as a bridge to walk across. She repeats the process till she has made the frame of her web, and then weaves in the radial spokes.

She goes round and round, from the centre to the outside of the frame and coats the last few spiral strands with gum from one of her spinnerets. Her feet are slightly greasy so that she doesn't stick to her own web. Then she sits, waiting patiently for some unwary insect to fly into her web and become entangled.

She pops out and seals its doom by trussing it in silk and

injecting it with poison – a specialised type of poison, which liquefies the victim so that she can eat it like soup.

Although there are several hundred different sorts of spider, we are only aware of the larger or more obvious. But some chase their prey, some dig pits and leap out at it, and one even builds her own bubble diving-bell and lives under water.

In a way, the tiny ones are more impressive. One scientist calculated that there were two-and-a-half million spiders on a single acre of field. The webs they spin would reach to the moon in ten days – if only they could be persuaded to spin them from end to end!

Imagine the havoc the insects they feed on would do, if it wasn't for these spiders. In the old days they were used medicinally, and a spider in a box hung round a child's neck was thought to cure malaria. If you swallowed one, wrapped in a raisin, your fever would abate and I knew a man who believed nothing would stop bleeding quicker than a spider's web clapped on the wound. Old wives' tales, perhaps.

But I, for one, would never kill a spider, and one day, I hope, a money spider will land on my hand while I am filling in my pools.

24. Don't confuse shooters with sportsmen

November 1, 1968

An exciting variety of duck visits our pool at this time of the year. Some migrate here from abroad, when our swallows and other summer migrants fly away to the south. Some leave the little pools and swamps and coppices where they go to breed in summer to spend their winter on lakes and reservoirs.

They can skulk by day in the centre of these lakes, out of range of sportsmen. At dusk they fly to feed in smaller pools and weedy streams, where they would be shot if they showed themselves when men could see to aim a gun.

I am very lucky. I live within a couple of miles – as the duck flies – of Blithfield reservoir. This is famous as a wintering ground for wild duck and the South Staffordshire Waterworks Company, who own it, issue permits to members of the West Midlands Bird Club to go there to watch the duck from 'hides'.

Blithfield is not just a reservoir of water. It is also a reservoir of wildfowl, many of which spill out into the surrounding countryside to visit smaller pools like ours.

The other day I was delighted to see that three pairs of shovellers had joined our other ducks. The females were dowdy brown, but a shoveller drake is a dandy of the feathered world; an extrovert with shining green head, white front and broad, flamboyant chestnut bellyband. He leers at you with roguish yellow eyes, but it is his bill that really gives the game away.

A huge bill, longer than his head and wide enough to scoop vast quantities of food. This living shovel seems too heavy for the bird and gives the head a knowing tilt. And it collects a perpetual dewdrop as it skims the surface of the water.

Shovellers are by no means the only interesting wildfowl that join our resident flock. Already this season we have had a pathetic little widgeon duck. Her feathers were ruffled and she walked with a limp carrying, I suppose, a load of lead shot fired at her from outside lethal range. She stayed for a day or so, feeding with our duck, and then she disappeared. I never discovered whether her wound had healed or if she crept away to die.

We get parties of teal, our smallest British duck, which de-

77

light us with displays of aerobatics so intricate and precise that the pilots at Farnborough look pallid amateurs by comparison.

Methods of shooting wildfowl have changed a lot since the war. And like many other changes, these have not been for the better. In the old days 'sportsmen' took great pride in giving their quarry a sporting chance. They regarded 'browning' easy birds as little short of poaching.

Whatever opinions may be about the ethics of killing for sport, the fact is that, from the quarry's point of view, the most important thing is not so much why men want to kill as how. The approved method of duck shooting in the old days was to attract ducks to small pools, once so common on farmland, by putting grain in shallow water. The duck soon found this on their nightly forays and then parties would literally drop-in for a feed as dusk was falling.

One, or at most two, sportsmen would hide by the pool and wait till a number of duck were feeding. A clap of hands would startle them into flight and offer a fleeting difficult shot at the retreating quarry. No shot was taken 'out of range' and the object was to give the birds a sporting chance by making things difficult for the man with the gun.

Nowadays many people describe themselves as 'shooters' instead of 'sportsmen' or 'guns'. To those not versed in country ways the distinction may seem merely academic, but there is a significant difference.

These modern shooters are interested only in the number of game they shoot. They line the banks of duck flighting ponds in hordes and fill the air with explosions the moment a bird comes over their horizon. It is massacre, by weight of firepower, and the birds stand about the same 'sporting' chance as a blade of grass does with a swarm of locusts.

Stragglers who see the fate of the vanguard veer off, but to this new breed of 'shooter' to be in sight is to be in shot. Many birds creep painfully away to die, like our little widgeon.

We are very lucky here, not only because we are near enough to Blithfield to get a constant stream of duck from the reservoir, but also in our neighbours. Trevor Jolliffe, whose field comes up to our pool, does not shoot at all, so our duck are safe from him. Edward Froggatt, on the other side of the lane, has old-fashioned standards of sportsmanship and does not believe in 'browning' his neighbour's birds.

So it is safe for me to keep a small flock of hand-reared mallard that grow as tame as barnyard ducks. I feed them by the window every morning and every evening, and we enjoy their gay colours and friendly calls and the patterns they make at sunset, flighting on and off the water. Because they are so tame, genuinely wild, wild duck sense their security and fly down to join them and eat at our expense.

I started with a score of mallard and a few odd species, like Carolina and mandarins and tufted. Now we get all sorts and there are often fifty or sixty feeding, fearless, within a few yards of the house. If a stranger comes, they are suspicious and take fright, so I don't think their tameness here makes them any easier target for the shooters.

25. The food of love

November 8, 1968

It was once fashionable for those who could afford it to forsake our shores for sunnier climes at the first whiff of November fog. Those who stayed behind got the best of the bargain. At no time of the year does the English countryside look lovelier.

Catches of watery autumn sun paint the bark of silver birches an iridescent white, adding emphasis to their gilded leaves. The bracken in our wood is richer red than the reddest headed showgirl and the oak leaves shade from sombre green to mellow gold. This is because all English oaks are not one species. Their acorns are of different shapes and their leaves decline and die over quite a lengthy period. They mingle with the leaves of ash and beech and holly and sycamore to weave a satisfying backcloth for meditation. Their colours are so much more inspiring than the transient brilliance of foreign shores.

The farm past our wood is a patchwork of rich ploughed earth and tawny stubble . . . a reminder that our harvest is in and that the rural rhythm is already begetting next year's plenty.

The unimaginative may regard these gorgeous autumn tints as no more than the symbols of death and decay. Withered leaves to them are only a prelude to the stark reality of ruthless winter.

But among those fading leaves are the fruits that fill the wood with life. This has been a marvellous year for acorns, some of which have fallen while others cling stubbornly aloft. We get very few rooks except when the acorns are ripe, when they fly here in flocks and blacken the crowns of the oaks. Then they steal off singly with their spoil, beaks ajar, down to the neighbouring turf.

Acorns are not the easiest things to carry in horny beaks, and they often drop them in mid-air. They don't bother to fly down to pick them up, but leave them to sprout where they fall while they return to plunder more.

As the acorns ripen, more and more are buffeted off by

hordes of jostling wood pigeons. They fall, unheeded, to lie among the leaves, but they don't remain unheeded long. Pheasants are everywhere, scratching like barnyard hens for grain. Grey squirrels appear, as if by magic, but it is a perilous place for them because I have to control their numbers for the safety of the smaller birds.

I have been so successful this year, that for the first time since we came a grand crop of hazel nuts has been left in peace to ripen. More nut bushes will sprout from those which survive and thicken the cover at the foot of the trees. This will provide additional retreat and food, making it even more attractive for more creatures in years to come.

The day will come when I shall have been more successful than I want and I shall be forced to sweat to make pleasant, open clearings in a jungle of plenty.

I can understand the attraction of acorns for birds because if they have a sense of taste at all, and I am not certain that they have, it must be a very different sense from ours. They love wheat and oats and seeds of flowers and weeds which would be insipid stuff to our palates. Perhaps their pleasure is triggered more by touch than taste.

But animals love acorns, too. I noticed almost a bucketful on the floor of a chicken coop and spent some time watching and waiting to see who had stored them there. My vigil was rewarded by the sight of a long-tailed woodmouse, struggling along a twig, holding in his mouth a huge acorn, twice the size of his head. He winkled his way through a mesh of wire netting and staggered across the floor to the corner. Then he placed his prize on top of the pile of food which would have done credit to a black market hoarder in time of war. His eyes will be dim and his whiskers grey long before he can consume half of it.

Acorns and hazel nuts are not the only attractions in our wood. This autumn juicy blackberries have survived right into November. Every wise countryman knows how dangerous it is to eat blackberries at this time of year because the devil puts his cloven hoof on them in October.

You only have to walk on any muddy ride in our wood to be convinced the story is true. There are clear imprints of cloven hooves on every patch of soggy ground. They are not footprints of the devil, though. They are tracks left by dainty fallow deer, who love blackberry fruits and leaves as well. They love acorns and beechmast and hazel nuts and I have been watching them idly eating the drying leaves of oak and damson as they flutter to the ground.

Last month we had about a dozen does, accompanied by a great tawny buck. He was groaning ceaseless challenges to his rivals because he had dedicated himself not to food, but love. When the does waxed fat and sleek on their gastronomic affluence, his surfeit of passion wasted him to a shadow of his former self and he paid dearly for his excesses.

A strange young buck invaded the wood. A mere adolescent stripling who would never have dared to show himself a few short weeks ago. He knew by instinct that the old buck had spent his powers and that he was no longer a match for the virility of youth.

So the intruder challenged him for possession of the herd and it was sad to see the old beast forced to slink abjectly away, humbled before his own harem. The young buck will be wise not to let his successes go to his head. He must not get ideas beyond his station.

A few barrow loads of brambles and a bellyful of acorns may well revitalise the old buck's powers before next mating season. This could give the next chapter a very different ending. The old rake may restore his self esteem by cutting the arrogance of youth down to its proper proportions.

26. *Fido gets his kicks with corn*

Poaching is a declining art because the urge to poach for food has gone and it is now fashionable to sit back and be amused instead of finding your own amusement. Although this has eased gamekeepers' night duties, they have to be far more vigilant by day than once they were. The odd sneak-thief taking pot-shots at pheasants from his car is fairly easy meat because he rarely has the guts to make a fight of it.

But innocent, doting dog lovers are often hard to convince that the Access to the Countryside Act does not give them the right to wander where they will. It is hardest of all to persuade them to keep their dogs under control in public open spaces, like Cannock Chase. They say that their dogs have wonderful fun chasing hares or deer or pheasants. It is obvious that nothing short of a catastrophic miracle would deliver the quarry to such pampered panting pets, so where is the harm?

Dog owners must realise that they have no right whatsoever to allow dear Fido to get his kicks from chasing deer. Although there may be no chance of the deer being caught, it might cross a road, cause an accident and probably be killed. Of the sixty or so deer killed by cars on the Chase last year, the majority had been driven from their natural grounds by people or dogs. In any case, there are rigid regulations to prevent owners allowing their dogs to disturb wildlife in public places.

On private land, which happens to include a large part of the Chase, it is no more lawful to allow dogs to harry game than it would be to invade a private garden and hunt the owner's cat. Apart from the purely legal aspect of ownership, there are very good reasons for keeping dogs under proper control in the country.

Most people rightly regard public open spaces as spare lungs for those confined to towns for most of their working lives. More and more countryside is being made available for public access and more and more people are learning to enjoy it to the full.

Bird watching clubs swell in numbers and membership and

groups of enthusiasts wander in autumn woods diligently seeking for new varieties of fungus. A tiring tramp across rough ground suddenly becomes worth all the discomfort for the sight of a green woodpecker probing the turf for ants, or a red squirrel shredding fire cones for their seeds.

Nothing is more beautiful than a party of fallow deer which have been taught by experience that men will do them no harm. I have proved for myself how easy this is to achieve. The deer in our wood used to be harried by dogs or peppered with shot the moment they showed their noses.

I am now in the wood every day, and several times a day. But I confine myself to the rides and do not disturb the areas where the deer lie-up. In four short years they have learned for themselves exactly where they will be safe, so I can now pass within a few yards without alarming them at all.

The lesson seems to be that the public who want to enjoy wildlife as well as views and fresh air, must respect the instincts of the creatures they wish to see. One rebel who flouts this code of practice, will cancel ten successes. I do not mean by this that I would like to ban dogs from open spaces or to insist they were tied to their owners with leads.

We have four dogs, an alsatian named Tough and three lurchers. Tough sleeps in our bedroom and all four spend their days in the comfort of my study or wandering with me in the woods outside. A dog's life, to them, is the luxury of human companionship and food – and discipline.

That is the secret. They learn as tiny puppies what things they may not chase. As soon as they can walk, they come with me to feed the stock, and I watch for the first moment it occurs to them what fun it would be to catch a duck or chicken. This is the instant that a handful of corn rattles round their ears. That is the moment they first hear my voice in wrath. The surprise is all they need to distract them and they associate the unpleasant sensation with their first thought of rioting. The surprise of those few grains of corn is more effective than an old-fashioned kick in the ribs!

Their training benefits me as much as them. We spend hours together in the woods, and I have learned to share their perceptive senses for the clues I might have missed. A twitching nose, delicately testing the breeze, often pin-points a pheasant that would otherwise have cowered unnoticed. Ears are cocked to warn of a deer's approach long before I could have possibly heard it myself.

The simple fact is that the initial discipline soon becomes automatic. Then I can take them wherever I like in the confidence that they will be my subtle second eyes helping me to enjoy the things I might never have seen for myself.

27. Wolf whistles in the wood

November 22, 1968

I used to enjoy observing the response of feminine guests to a sound that was once common in our wood. It was a delightfully musical whistle, limpid and provocative; varied but always tuneful. It was obvious to the most unperceptive ears.

I analysed my guests' reactions with the dispassionate objectivity of a dedicated naturalist. The instincts of some women were obviously stirred by the first notes of music. Yet they tried to bluff me that the wood was silent as a morgue. Some unleashed a flood of small talk in a conscious effort to drown extraneous sound. Others blushed and fell silent, eager to hear the encore more acutely.

I knew that the stimulus that provoked such unpredictable reactions was simply the song of a bird. The bird was fairly common in our wood but rare enough in areas without a lot of trees to be unfamiliar to most of our guests. It was all too easy for those who did not know to mistake that tuneful sound for a human wolf whistle of extrovert admiration.

Some took it as a compliment and others as an insult. The wise feigned ignorance until they could unmask the author. The reactions I observed gave wonderful clues to female character.

All that, unfortunately, is a thing of the past. The bird that whistled with such seduction in our wood was a nuthatch. A smallish bird with long, strong beak, rather like a dowdy kingfisher. The crown of his head and the whole of his back was greyish, where his rival would be brilliant iridescent 'kingfisher' blue. The nuthatch had a black eye-stripe instead of chestnut, and faded chestnut where the kingfisher's underside was flamboyant brown.

For the first two years we were here at Goat Lodge never a day passed without seeing and hearing nuthatches. They came three or four at a time in winter to gorge on the fat at the bird table.

They clung to the bark of trees with the graceful ease of squirrels and rushed down head first as easily as a clown in a circus. And like clowns, they seemed to enjoy playing jokes on our guests, teasing them with whistles of pretended admiration.

Then, gradually, a couple of years ago it dawned on us that they were getting rarer in our wood. It is easy to be fairly precise when strange birds come. We always look forward to marking the date on the calendar when we see our first swallow or house martin, or hear the first cuckoo of the season. It is much more difficult to be exact about the date that one of the flock goes absent.

I think the first thing we noticed consciously was that manners had improved at the bird table. Birds that make bold wolf whistles at strangers are predictably rude over food. They strut around the table, threatening lesser fry like tits and robins with the spiteful daggers they use as beaks.

When two nuthatches arrive together each stakes a claim with more rough vigour than two starlings. We began to realise that our fat vanished with less uncouth greed and we thought that the nuthatches had simply moved to other parts of the wood.

They nest in holes, like tits, and are very clever about making sure their front door is exactly the right size. They do so by choosing a hole already hollowed in a tree – perhaps by a woodpecker the year before – and then they plaster the hole up with mud, reducing the diameter till it might be tailormade. This leaves no doubt to the observant where they are nesting.

Two years ago was the first time we had not found a nest in the wood and we haven't seen or heard a nuthatch since. At first I thought the malady must be very local and I constantly expected overspill from lucky areas round about to replace our falling population, but I haven't seen any in neighbouring woods – and it is almost impossible not to hear their constant whistle if they are there.

I mentioned it to several friends in the West Midland Bird Club to try to discover how widespread is this dramatic slump in nuthatch numbers. In every case, the reply was that there are plenty in other woods. Then usually a chink of doubt peeps through as an afterthought – 'I think,' they add!

Certainly a close friend living by the wood at Hoar Cross, seven or eight miles away, has had the same experience and noticed that his hordes of nuthatches have disappeared as well. We have puzzled our heads for the reason.

There has been no hard winter; they are a species living so

much in woodland, especially old woodland, that they are less likely than most to have been poisoned by agricultural sprays or other works of man. So far as I know, there has been no great bulge in the population of stoats or cats or crows or owls which might conceivably have decimated them, nor has there been a decline in the area of the woodland where they loved to live.

Their disappearance is a mystery but I hope they will soon return. I miss the fun of reading the character of our friends from their reactions to the flattery of the nuthatch's song.

28. Defeated by the untytumps

December 13, 1968

My wife has green fingers. The flowers and shrubs in her garden are happy and take pride in flourishing for her. In the space of four short years, she has changed a wilderness of scrub into beds and lawns which seem to have been there as long as our old house.

The green finger business is not just luck. She spends hours weeding and hoeing and daydreaming of the exact spot where her latest (or next!) acquisition will look its best. Above all, she believes it is important to keep as good a table for her plants as she does for us. Every weed heaved out goes on to the compost heap for a year and then returns to the flower beds as rich humus.

She supplements this compost with generous loads of rotted farmyard muck, in the belief that you get nothing out of life you don't put in – and plants only grow well if you feed them. The snag is that she doesn't only feed the plants. She feeds the worms as well.

Where there are plenty of worms, especially on the edge of old woodland like ours, there are plenty of moles to catch them. Fond of animals as she is, she does draw the line at moles in the garden. A molehill on the lawn is a mountain to her and she says they maliciously choose her favourite plants to undermine with their tunnels.

A local farmer advised her to stick a thorny rose briar down all the tunnels she could find. He assured her that they would rather starve than face the prickles, and that thorny tunnels would force them to find pastures new. But our succulent loamy compost produced five-star worms, which no mole could resist. They simply dug new tunnels a few inches away from those she had stuffed with briars.

The soil they excavated had to go somewhere else, so they left a larger crop of molehills on the lawn than ever. Someone said: 'Put a moth ball down each hole. Moles can't bear the stink of moth balls.'

Nor can I. So feeling guilty of cruelty to dumb animals, I

tried it. The cure was worse than the disease because they dug new tunnels much further from the original than before. Instead of the edge of the lawn being defaced by molehills, the centre looked like a desert strewn with pyramids.

The alternative was traps, but trapping moles is a specialist art which went out of fashion with moleskin waistcoats. I take great pride in catching every rat that ventures over our boundary, but I confess that I should never make a decent living from moleskins if they were worth as much as mink. They ran less risk from my traps than I run every time I cross a city street.

We know when we're beaten so I admit we've adopted a defensive policy. We leave them alone unless they really provoke us beyond endurance. This is not as silly as it sounds. Moles are perfect digging machines. Their skulls are long and their snouts pointed to streamline their progress through the soil. Their claws are as sharp as pickaxes and their leathery paws can dig like navvies' shovels.

They don't waste energy showering cascades of spoil behind them, but seem almost to swim through the ground. Putting out their forepaws like the first graceful movement of the breast stroke, they heave themselves through the earth, leaving a tunnel almost the same size as their bodies.

It used to be thought that moles had to hunt each worm and that the nourishment they got from it only just replaced the energy expended to catch it. So moles were supposed to be so hungry that they had to dig constantly for food and Shropshire people still call them 'unts' – which is dialect for 'wants'. Because of this, in Shropshire, a molehill is an 'untytump'.

Scientists have now exploded this myth. They have shown that the whole network of underground tunnels is really an enormous trap. Worms, digging through the soil, fall into the tunnels and the mole doesn't have to dig for them at all. All he has to do is to patrol his burrows and reap the rich harvest, which falls down in front of his nose.

It is easy to see this in our garden because, year after year, the moles use the same main runs from the wood to the garden and on to the paddock. At the moment, they are 'working' new ground near the pool and they have thrown up a whole range of new molehills, where they can do no harm to anyone.

Meanwhile, we take great care not to disturb the ground in the garden and crush their tunnels in. If we do, there will be a new crop of molehills left where they repair the damage.

We find it much pleasanter to leave well alone than having to mess about with traps or briars or moth balls. And so, I expect, do the moles.

29. Oh! to stay in England!

December 27, 1968

I am old-fashioned enough to believe that nowhere in the world is as good as England and am always careful to put English, not British, against my name in hotel registers. Otherwise, I might be confused with foreigners from over the borders of Scotland and Wales.

The only time I visited France I found the food messed-up and over-rated and the buildings in Paris looked as dingy and grubby as the older parts of Brum. Even the stars at the Folies Bergères were not a patch on my nostalgic memories of the pre-war Windmill girls.

However biased and reactionary it may seem, I am violently hostile to the current gimmickry of putting our clocks in step with those on the Continent. Looked at under the glaring lights of Westminster, I suppose dark mornings are no more dreary than light ones.

But plenty of antiquated countrymen like me would welcome the chance of explaining to M.P.s our views on groping about like nightowls, when civilised tradition tells us that dawn should long since have broken. It seems unnatural to us to hear the first cock crow after breakfast, and our dogs are obviously convinced that our clocks have started to run on wheels.

They expect to be taken up the wood as soon as I get up and they look forward to stretching in luxury by the radiator when we come back for winter breakfast.

That isn't possible without a flashlight in these topsy-turvy times. Although their behaviour is impeccable in broad daylight, they are not a bit above sneaking off on poaching forays if they think it too dark for me to notice. So we have to have breakfast first, and then there is time to throw some corn to the fowls before they have even come down from roost.

Wild duck are crepuscular creatures that love to feed at dawn and dusk. They have come up the paddock by the time I have fed the poultry, babbling among themselves about the maize and barley they know is in my bucket. Their broad bills are sensitive enough to dibble in mud and sift out the hard grains of edible corn and the horny forms of water insects. So they easily find the food I throw down in the grass before it is really light enough to see.

The dogs wait for the moment I finish feeding – and then they give me no peace. Strangers might imagine that they had been chained for six months to a barrel and had no exercise at all. They chase each other in circles; they leap over the fence into the spinney and back, as if propelled by purple hearts, and fetch up, panting, by the paddock gate.

Their one aim in life, it seems, is to escape into the wood. Yet, the moment we get through the gate and the world is theirs, their exuberance shells off and they come to heel as naturally as shadows.

The winter birch trees look lovely in the half-light, especially if there is just a catch of mist. Their subtle colours turn to gold the moment the first rays light them up.

If there has been a touch of frost the dullest eyes can see where the deer have crossed the ride, and which gaps in the fence are used by hares or badgers or foxes.

There are enormous varieties of food in the part of the wood where the young pine trees grow, so that the tracks converge there like main roads. I imagine all sorts of creatures jostling there for a place, at dead of night, because there are usually revellers straggling home when we arrive.

The veil of mist, which cloaks the trees, magnifies things larger than life. The pheasants clattering down from their perches look as big as peacocks, and our bantam, crowing on the bird table, is clear and musical, half a mile away up the wood. The sheep, two or three fields away across the plough, might be just behind the briar patch.

Unluckily, we live just under the air route from Elmdon to Manchester. I often find it almost impossible to make a sound recording of foxes or bird song without the rumble of aircraft as background accompaniment. It is a horrible, intrusive dirge and I loathe the engineers who are clever enough to make flying machines but too incompetent to silence them.

Misty dawns in the wood emphasise this because quiet, then, is almost tangible. Aircraft are grounded, drivers can't see yet to plough so are greasing their tractors in the warmth of the shed, and concentrations of motor cars crawl along the faraway main roads.

So there is no sound in our wood that our ancestors couldn't have heard centuries ago. A dog barking down in the village, a cowman rounding-up his herd, or birds that have always sung there. It is a wonderful silence for such an over-crowded little island, and it highlights the fact that our trees are richer and our grass is greener and our birdsong sweeter than anywhere else in the world.

The deeper my content, the more I dislike those who want us English Jacks to get in step with other folk. So, at a minute to midnight on Tuesday (*not* at twenty-three hours fifty-nine minutes!) I shall make my New Year resolution to applaud everyone who wants to keep England as she is.

30. Teamwork foxed the fox

January 3, 1969

Like most people who are stirred by primitive things, I can never resist the thrills of playing with fire or water. At our last house the mill stream ran through the garden and had once been diverted by a sluice to flow through a pleasant pool in front of the window. The brickwork of this sluice had rotted and tumbled in by the time we arrived so that the brook shied away to run through a ford out of sight of the house, just beyond our boundary.

All that remained of the pool was a stinking, gnat-ridden swamp. The cheapest cure would have been to clay-puddle the gap where the sluice had been, fill in the pool with soil and sow a lawn instead.

However nice a lawn may look, nothing gives a garden such charm as a sheet of water, with a few wild duck to add colour and movement. The prospect of restoring the flow to give back life to the old pool was more than I could resist.

We did not begin to enjoy ourselves until we had done the donkey work of shifting tons of silt and rubbish. Then we slithered about in wellingtons, rebuilding the old sluice and fitting a sluice-gate of stout elm planks that will survive for generations under water.

We discovered that there had once been not one pool but two, at different levels, so we strengthened the old dividing wall with concrete and cleaned out the brick culvert, which returned the water to the brook.

It was a labour of love. I shall never forget the thrill of seeing water first trickle back into the pool and wondering if the dam at the other end would hold. It took two or three days to fill, but on the second night we heard the delighted cries of water hens, which afterwards stayed to breed. The joy we got after that obliterated all memories of our hard labour. I spent happy hours placing rocks and persuading waterfalls to play their loveliest tunes.

I missed the brook when we moved house because I'd grown so accustomed to falling asleep to its lullaby. Although our pool here is much bigger, it is quieter because it is fed by hidden springs and water which only drains from the wood. There wasn't much to see when we first came because a dense reed bed shielded the water from the house.

When the mechanical digger arrived to dig a septic tank and level the site for the extension we built, I got the chap to push the reeds up to one end of the pool and bulldoze a patch where the water could lap right up to the edge of the paddock.

Our friends thought this an extravagant conceit, but the cost was hidden in the work on the house and we were careful never to enquire too deeply, so that our conscience never troubled us. Last spring we bulldozed out an island which will enchant us for years for less than the price of the holiday we didn't take.

Although there is not enough running water to play tunes, the problems it poses are quite as interesting as our first pool. It was originally made by damming a little valley to form a large collecting basin. It was built long before the days of mechanical diggers by men with picks and spades and muscle. They didn't make it to amuse themselves, but to provide a water supply for the farm just down the lane.

There is still an ancient stone conduit under the field, but it has been dry since a modern supply of water was laid on in the taps.

In wet weather my problem is to stop too much water coming in from the wood, because it washes down leaves and silt which steal the pool's depth. In frost or drought, on the other hand, I try to improve the flow.

In order to get this control I opened up the ditches in the wood except at one spot, which I dammed entirely, leaving only a small pipe at the bottom of the ditch. In times of drought, there is always a trickle through this pipe from a small spring at the far end of the wood. When there is too much rain I block it up altogether so that the water backs-up high enough to flow away at right angles into a stream about half a mile away.

In frost, the water from the wood is still running into the pool long after the surface has frozen, so that it is warmer than it would have been and there is always an open patch at the inflow.

At this time, the duck have to work to help themselves. They mass together wherever the water is most sheltered and warm and some sit on the edges of the ice. The rest swim ceaselessly round to prevent their patch of open pool from freezing. When

1. The author with his three lurchers and German short-haired pointer.

2. The drake's dark plumage will soon moult out to gorgeous black and white.

3. Pied wagtails in the garage.

4. Victim of some unknown litter-lout.

5.   A ringed bat.

6.   A polecat-ferret, sniffing freedom.

7. Phil Drabble expressing his *melophilia*.

8. A young cuckoo.

9. A crafty fox can outwit the hunt.

10. Winter birch trees look lovely in half-light.

11. Blue-tits on a nut feeder.

12. The common toad.

13.   A gyr falcon.

14.   Bill the Badger.

15. The willow warbler.

16. Miss Roe calls at the study.

17.   A long-tailed tit with chicks in the nest.

18.   The weasel is one of the shyest animals.

19.   Duck on the frozen pool.

20.   Bill the boar with two badger sows.

21.   A sparrow hawk.

22.   The lurchers in mock combat.

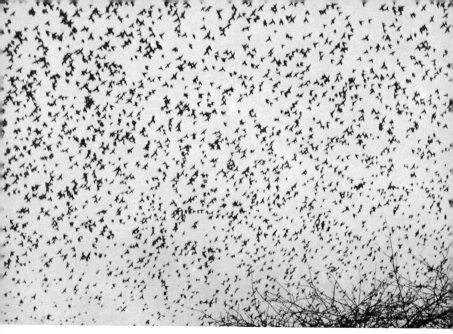

23. Starlings flock together.

24. Tick points at Miss Roedoe.

they get tired, they swap places with ducks that were resting on the ice.

It is a marvellous example of teamwork to beat a common foe, for they keep their bit of pool free of ice when the rest is frozen several inches thick. Then, if a fox or cat comes too near, they can retreat from attack to the safety of their icy water.

This frigid game of ducks-and-drakes may not give them as much sheer fun as I get, but theirs is a game of life and death.

31. Bawled out by a toffee-nosed tart

January 17, 1969

One of the unfulfilled ambitions of my childhood was to own a horse. I wanted a pony more than anything in the world, but my father was a very un-horsey man. He said that ponies were all right in the holidays, but who did I think was going to look after it when I was away at school? And that was that.

A break came in the clouds when I struck up a friendship with the sons of the colliery manager of Hilton Main, which is one of the latest Midland pits to be condemned to closure. In those days, ponies were bought wild off the mountains of Wales, or from the New Forest, and kept on the pit bank until the blacksmith had time to break them in.

Among the perks of pit managers' sons was the choice of un-limited ponies to ride in the holidays. There was only one con-dition. The boys had to catch-up the wild youngsters and break them in for themselves. There was no nonsense like letting the boss's kids spoil ponies which had cost good money to train.

I was enthralled by the prospect when they invited me to join their circus, but I knew, by instinct, that it was vital to keep it dark at home. If my father found out, he would have nipped the friendship smartly in the bud.

Anyone who has watched Wild West on television (and it is depressingly difficult to avoid it) will have a fair idea of the process involved. When 'our' ponies were quiet enough to let us handle them, and would wear a bridle, we tried to ride them like bucking broncos in a rodeo.

All difficulty is a matter of degree, and professional cowboys would doubtless have rated our ponies tame. To us, they were fiery steeds and the fact that we had no saddles added to the difficulty of sticking on their backs for long. It taught us to fall without hurting ourselves much, because it was far too hazardous to lie there, waiting for a non-existent ambulance man. Our ponies were liable to show their contempt of kids who fell off by aiming a playful kick at them next time round the field. So it was vital to make yourself scarce as soon as you could.

In retrospect, I can see how wise my father would have been to stop us, if he'd known. As it was, the ponies soon got over their worst stage and we struck up some degree of mutual respect and affection.

This inflated our over-confidence and we decided to take them fox hunting. Not the pukkah thing, of course, with pink coats and toffee noses, but the more informal business of early morning cub hunting. It is no coincidence that this was the first and only time that I have ventured, mounted, on to the hunting field.

I have often wondered what the members thought when they were joined by three tearaway kids, on unkempt ponies, equipped with bits and bridles, but little else. No saddles or stirrups for the mounts, or respectable gear for us.

We didn't tie red ribbon in their tails to show they were liable to kick, because it was a convention we'd never even heard of. The moment hounds came near, our nags let fly, and the only compensation was that they hadn't even been shod, so that their heels at least lacked the lethal finality of cold steel.

The Master nearly had apoplexy at such behaviour by un-invited guests, so we retreated to the far corner of the field, where we could watch what went on and giggle a little to give us courage. Long practice had taught us to dodge those flying heels, so we rated his foxhounds fairly stupid to have come within range; but the instant they found their fox, there was no time for theorising.

At the first burst of hound music, the more intrepid heroes of the hunt put their horses at the nearest fence and dis-appeared from view. The remainder made for an open gateway and filed politely through, with no unseemly bunching.

We had no intention of missing any fun. Indeed, we had no choice because our ponies were naturally competitive and had the bad manners to push themselves to the fore whenever pos-sible. My two friends had had enough practice to make them pretty competent riders, so they dived unceremoniously to the head of the queue – that was the last I saw of them.

My betters often told me that I resembled a sack of potatoes on a horse and I freely admit I had about as much control. My pony succeeded in sandwiching himself between two elegant ladies, slap in the middle of a gateway, and nearly tipped them off. He managed to squeeze beneath them unscathed and cele-brated his triumph by kicking his heels in their horses' faces.

This tipped me off and left me sitting in the mud at their

feet, a helpless target for the stream of unladylike abuse that huntin' women murmur on such occasions. From their horses' haughty heights, those women left me in no doubt how impudent and ill-mannered I was to dream of bringing my scruffy little nag in their vicinity.

Breeches drenched with the impact of sodden clay are not conducive to swift or telling repartee, so it didn't even occur to me to inform them that their distaste was mutual.

I picked myself up and slunk off on foot in a fruitless search for my runaway mount. By the end of that miserable morning, during which he was always a frustrating field ahead, I was firmly convinced that there is nothing more stupid than a horse except mugs like me, who climb upon his back.

32. The critical days

Whatever the weather man says, I have a theory that the last few days in January are critical for the rest of the winter. I regard them as sort of St Swithin's days and reckon that if we get much heavy snow before the end of next week, we are probably in for a long hard spell.

I have none of the scientific gadgetry of the Met. Office and may well be as inaccurate as their forecasts, but at least I have taken precautions.

For several weeks I have cut all the scraps of fat from the dog meat, melted it down and stored it in hunks the size of the saucepan. These are now festooned round the house and garden, like parcels on a Christmas tree. If we do get an old-fashioned winter, I've got plenty of replacements.

The birds that come display disconcertingly human weakness. The easier things are, the more pugnacious and aggressive their behaviour. If we get a really prolonged spell of hard weather, it will blunt the edge of their belligerence, despite the fact that it will then be even more vital to corner every available morsel of food.

Our wood is a paradise for a great variety of small birds, including six different varieties of tits. The commonest are in our picture section. These are so common that it is easy to notice just how blue blue tits can be. Their breasts are a superb shade of greenish yellow and the feathers on their wings and the crown on their heads are the smokey-blue of fragrant wood smoke.

Although the great and blue tits are the commonest and boldest of the family, we get coal tits, marsh tits and willow tits as well. The coal tits are easy to distinguish. Even smaller than blue tits, they are less gaudy. A subtle olive-grey back, buff breast and black head, with a prominent white stripe on the nape of the neck.

It is this stripe which distinguishes them from marsh and willow tits. He is a better naturalist than I am who can spot the difference between marsh and willow varieties, even a few yards away, except by voice.

Both are brown with black skull cap and chin, though the willow tit has an even sootier black cap than the marsh tit, which is glossy by comparison. It also has a light streak on the edge of the wing feathers, though I find it hard to be certain of this unless I can almost touch it.

The one distinguishing feature is the voice, but even that is difficult for unmusical ears like mine, except by direct comparison. The truth is that marsh and willow tits are so alike that their shades of difference are only of academic interest to dedicated bird watchers who 'collect' different species on their check-lists with the acquisitive zeal of train spotters.

To me both are among the most attractive and welcome visitors who call and I don't give a rap which is which.

All five species – the great, blue, coal, marsh and willow – come to the fat in winter and when times are really hard, they sink their differences and eat in amity. But the real place to get the best effect is on the honeysuckle berries.

Outside the kitchen window is a thick honeysuckle hedge, as English as roses, in flower and fragrance, on summer evenings; hospitable with crimson berries, in autumn. All sorts of birds come there to feast, especially coal and marsh (or willow) tits. Bullfinches and greenfinches join them and, occasionally, goldfinches – the lovely seven-coloured linnets of my Black Country boyhood.

The coal and marsh tits take pride of place for me. The crimson berries are the perfect foil for the subdued richness of their plumage.

Until I put out fat to attract them, the whole tribe forage among the birch trees in the wood. Silver birch is considered by foresters to be a noxious weed. It has no great economic value, so its beauty counts for nothing in hard cash. Whatever its worth to man, it is rich in food for birds. They love its seeds, the insects that live on its leaves and the grubs which take up residence in its rotten heart at the end of its short life.

All this autumn, there have been parties of long-tailed tits in the birches along the rides. They are easily distinguished from other small birds by the exceptional length of their tails. Their plumage is grey and white and pink and they spend the winter in family parties. Their flight is fragile, their voices tiny, and they give the impression they are too dainty to live.

I am sad to say that this diagnosis is all too near the bone. In hard frost, their long tails often freeze to the twigs and they have to pluck themselves free, leaving their tails, or perish.

They don't come to the fat, so starve if the supply of insects dries up, and their bodies are too tiny to maintain the warmth of life in very bitter weather.

So I trust my fears of a hard winter are misplaced. I would rather watch a family of long-tailed tits, dining on the birch trees, than have front seat at the ringside for the swaggering brawls of commoner species on the fat.

33. *Anthony, my uncle's toad*

January 31, 1969

Not everyone is as fond of toads as my uncle, who was a country doctor with a large practice in Wiltshire. He was such a serious, bearded, bespectacled fellow that his patients could never imagine him making time to bother about a pet.

Yet his toad, Anthony, who lived in the conservatory next to the surgery, was the apple of his eye. There was plenty of food there for him because my uncle would allow no one to treat the plants, even with the old-fashioned relatively harmless sprays of those days, lest Anthony be injured by eating a poisoned fly.

Every Victorian conservatory had geraniums and carnations and begonias which were rich in insect life but Anthony could not have survived there for more than twenty years if his digestion had been impaired by eating doped food. His flies were fat and juicy. They were as fit and healthy as members of a doctor's household ought to be.

When I went to stay during my summer holidays I was allowed to join my uncle after supper to watch him feed his pet. Because there was enough natural food to nourish an army of toads, there was really no necessity to feed him artificially at all. But my uncle used to amuse himself by taking a very long pair of surgical forceps. He caught the largest, noisiest bluebottle on the window pane and offered it to his toad.

It looked as tempting as the exotic flies on fishermen's hats and he accompanied its buzzing with a peculiar sizzling sound which he made through his teeth as grooms do when they are fettling horses. It was a penetrating hiss and within a few moments the old toad would waddle out of the crevice below the floor where he spent the day.

His throat throbbed and his unblinking eye fixed the bluebottle with a menacing stare from a range of an inch or so. Suddenly Anthony's tongue would shoot out too rapidly for the eye to follow. When it returned, the fly had gone.

I was enthralled by the degree of mutual understanding between my uncle and his pet because it disproved the theory that was current at the time. Scientists were trying to prove that such creatures as toads had no intelligence and were incapable of conscious action. They claimed that they were motivated by complicated reflexes which triggered them off mechanically, as current starts an electric motor.

To prove the point, one scientist put a fly inside a glass test tube and presented it to a toad which behaved exactly as Anthony did to the flies on the end of my uncle's forceps. There was the same deliberate focus to gauge the precise range. The tongue shot out with invisible speed and the toad's throat distended visibly as he 'swallowed' the fly. The only difference was that the fly was still in the test tube!

The experiment so appealed to my sense of humour that I was tempted to try the joke on Anthony and went out on the downs at the back of the house to catch a glow-worm. That evening, I sneaked out to the conservatory with my test tube to see if he would perform a widow's cruse act.

I wanted to see how often he would fool himself that he had swallowed the glow-worm before he discovered it was still as good as new, safe in the test tube.

Unfortunately, my uncle arrived before I reached a definite conclusion and his sense of humour was kinder than mine. He left me in no doubt that schoolboy visitors must treat his pet with due respect, and he removed my glow-worm from its glass sanctuary on the end of his forceps. The next time Anthony gulped, the lump in his throat was no illusion.

The life span of twenty years may seem a lot for so small a creature, but there are longer-lived toads than that. One reason is that they have an ingenious mechanism which protects them from most of their enemies.

When a toad is frightened or hurt, its skin which is rough with hundreds of tiny pimples, exudes a milky fluid. This contains *bufotalin* and *bufogin* which act as a poison to its enemies, slowing down their heart rate and affecting their central nervous system.

Dogs, cats, stoats and rats froth at the mouth if they bite a toad and do not come for a second helping. Scientists who experimented with *bufotalin* discovered that a minute dose caused temporary paralysis on part of the tongue.

In theory, a creature which is so distasteful to its enemies, can live for twenty years and lay as many as 6,000 eggs in a season, should multiply exceedingly. You might fear such hordes of toads that the Egyptians' plague of frogs would seem a gentle April shower.

The controlling factor that prevents this population explosion is the greenbottle fly. It looks like an ordinary bluebottle that has dolled itself up in shining green armour. When it is ready to breed, it lays its eggs on the back of a toad. The larvae hatch out and the maggots crawl up the toad's nostrils and literally eat him alive from inside his skull.

It is one of nature's most ruthless methods of population control and Anthony never realised his luck in having my uncle to pamper him.

34. Follow my leader

February 7, 1969

Our clay land has been so heavy and squelchy this wet winter that the gateways are a sea of glutinous mud which threatened to steal my wellingtons and strip me to my stockinged feet.

Despite theoretically good growing weather, there hasn't been much grass and cattle have spent hours browsing round the hay racks or waiting in the gateways for their daily ration of corn or cake. At first glance, they seem casual about where and when they feed and how they go from hay rack to gate and back. A closer examination will show what an ordered, well-disciplined community they are.

Because of the wet weather their tracks across the field have worn away the grass till snaky brown paths stand out as vivid as varicose veins. Each beast takes precisely the same route to the gate as the trail blazed by its fellows and keeps to it so accurately that the followers literally tread in the footsteps of their leader. They not only wear the same path but cut deep ruts in it like impressions of human feet on the stone of ancient castle steps.

When the parkland next to our wood was reclaimed for agriculture, it became clear that his habit is not confined to domestic cattle. The park once consisted of eight hundred acres of grass and reed and bracken, crossed by two brooks and dotted with small woods and clumps of trees. It had never been ploughed in living memory but grazed by cattle and sheep and goats and deer.

The cattle cut the same sort of tracks across it as they have done this winter in the fields. Because they grazed there for so many generations these paths stood out bold as watercourses cut in a relief map. They were used by the cattle only to get from one grazing area to another – and then they spread out to feed. Almost everything else used them too and I often saw deer and foxes and badgers running the tracks originally made by cows.

Then the clumps of trees were cut down and burned, the whole park criss-crossed with drains and the surface ploughed. The landscape was unrecognisable because the clear pattern of woods and copses was obliterated, leaving more than a square mile prairie of plough. There were no cattle to redefine their territory because now there was no grazing.

I found the footmarks of deer and foxes and hares in the mud along the brook-sides showing where they passed from one block of ploughland to the next. It gradually dawned on me that these crossings were sited exactly where they had been when the park was green and cattle had grazed there.

As time went on paths began to join one crossing place to the next, fainter than those cut by the hooves of heavy cattle but definite for all that. They too followed the traditional lines although there were no landmarks left to guide them, nor was it possible for them to have been marked out by scent trails because the top spit of turf where countless feet had trod had been buried a foot deep by the plough.

I tried in vain to decipher what it is that enables animals to choose the line of these specific tracks on a featureless landscape. The task would be quite beyond our effete human sense, as prisoners escaping the gaol at Dartmoor have often discovered to their cost. They simply wander in circles until they are captured.

I found this out for myself when I was once caught in the fog in the centre of a hundred-acre field. When I felt I was going a bit too much to the right I corrected my path, or so I thought! Within seconds, I was hopelessly lost and even when I came to the fence I didn't know whether to turn to left or right.

It is chastening to speculate how stupid animals might think I was.

Last autumn we were filming my tame badger and carried him to a patch of woodland which gave us the background we wanted to show. It was about a quarter of a mile from his sett and since he is very short-sighted and I had carried him all the way he could not have known whether 'home' was to the north or south.

After a while, he got bored with us. The ground was uneven and covered in brambles and bilberries and trees so that there was no possibility of his seeing the way he wanted to go even if he had not been so myopic. Yet he suddenly set off at a canter for home as accurately as if he had been piloted by a compass.

The wind was blowing from him towards the sett so he couldn't have been guided by scent. The two sow badgers who are his companions were curled up asleep so there was no question of their helping him even with his acute hearing.

It could, of course, have been memory. He feeds in the wood at night and may well know it like the back of his paw. But even if he does he would be no better off than I was in the hundred-acre field because there was nothing to give him a clue of direction.

I think it was more likely to be some instinct far beyond our understanding, an instinct possessed by animals both wild and domestic, which is far too subtle for our jaded human senses.

When paths made by cattle are obliterated by the plough and the area later repopulated by creatures that have never set foot there before, they remake the ancient ways as accurately as cartographers drawing a map. Although we know their senses are more acute than ours, we still haven't scratched the surface of their instincts.

Perhaps they possess a tenuous memory which not only spans their life but can bridge the generations to give them contact with the future and the past.

35. Pity the poor falcon!

February 14, 1969

A recent advertisement in a glossy, sporting magazine offered six species of hawk or falcon for sale. Three were definitely foreign species, which must have been imported because they are not found wild in this country.

Kestrels and buzzards were prefixed 'German', presumably to show that they had been imported, too, and the origin of goshawks, said to be expected soon, was unspecified.

British kestrels and buzzards and goshawks are all on our schedule of protected birds because, like other British birds of prey, they have been seriously threatened with extinction. For two hundred years they were shot on sight by many game-keepers, who classed them as vermin for daring to kill for food the pampered pheasants their masters shot for sport.

By the time sporting opinion became enlightened and realised that the countryside is large enough for hawks as well as game, the perils of poisonous pesticides were more deadly than the gun, so rigid protection is still essential.

Hawks and falcons would not be imported if there were not a ready market, but no field sport is more wrapped in glamour and mystique than falconry. Before shotguns were invented, it was the perquisite of nobility. There was a rigid sliding scale of class, which laid down which species of hawk a man might own. Only a king could keep a gyr falcon, a peregrine was for an earl, a merlin for a lady, a goshawk for a yeoman and, at the bottom of the scale, a priest could have a sparrow-hawk.

For some years I received an annual invitation to go grouse hawking on the Long Mynd, in Shropshire. My host has now moved to Ireland but, in those days, some of the best falconers from all over the world congregated in his isolated little game-keeper's cottage at the centre of the Midland moor.

He was a perfectionist and everything had to be right. The weather clear, the hawks fit and the wind not too strong. I shall never forget the first time I went. We walked through knee-high heather for what seemed like hours. My host, who had no blue blood in his veins, so far as I know, carried a gyr falcon fit for a king on his gloved fist.

It wore a hood, to defer the excitement of seeing its quarry till all was ready. A pair of soft leather jesses were tied to its legs to control it and its slightest movement produced a piercing, musical tinkle from its tiny falcon's bell.

When at last we paused, my host unhooded his falcon with reverent ceremony. The bird's huge eyes scanned the horizon for a few seconds, to get her bearings, then she shook her feathers and launched herself into space. She flew quite low and straight till she eventually shrank from view in the direction of Wales.

I watched aghast, certain in my mind that this was the last we should see of the noble bird. Nobody else seemed to worry. They simply stood still and waited.

Presently somebody spotted a speck in the sky about the size of a sparrow, soaring like a glider on the thermals. Instead of eloping for ever to freedom, as she easily could, the gyr falcon had returned to supervise our every movement from on high.

A brace of pointers were sent forward and we followed them across the heather. At last the dogs froze like statues, 'pointing' at a covey of grouse, crouching out of sight ahead. The speck in the sky, which had almost circled out of sight again, drifted back overhead and it was obvious that the gyr falcon knew the significance of the 'point'.

As soon as he saw she was ready, my host rushed forward and flushed the grouse which flew off for a distant patch of bracken. Grouse are such strong fliers and the falcon was so far aloft that pursuit seemed pointless.

She took a few short strokes and almost closed her wings. There was no real impression of speed, until I suddenly *heard* her fall. The wind through her feathers made the hissing sound I hadn't heard since bombs were falling in the war. The speed with which she caught up with those grouse was truly miraculous, but even so, they were too cunning for her and dived to safety in the bracken.

She was travelling so fast that she had to go into a vertical climb, shooting up perhaps a hundred feet, before she stalled. Then she returned to her pitch aloft and waited for us to flush more quarry for her.

My host, who trained that hawk, literally spent his whole summer dedicated to his birds. He was not interested in catching grouse, which in any case was such a rare event that he celebrated it by cracking a bottle of champagne whenever a hawk succeeded. His pleasure was to train hawks well enough to show him the sport that had been reserved for kings in olden times. It was such a demanding task that few people in any age have had the time or means to do it well.

Now it is suddenly becoming popular. Many people have seen the demonstrations of flying hawks free at the annual Game Fair and the glamour has fired their imagination.

All sorts of unsuitable people, with neither enough facilities nor expertise, are clamouring for a hawk. Falcons have suddenly become big business. Last week, a dealer in Penkridge had £250 worth stolen and there was a recent spate of raids on zoos for birds of prey.

The man whose advertisement I saw told me that he had imported fifty at Christmas, although one in five had died before he could sell it. It isn't the quarry I pity because few people buying these hawks will have the skill to get them fit enough to fly.

It is the hawks I am so sorry for, because I believe that, for most of them, their capture is their death sentence. They will fret out their hearts in captivity, victims not of deliberate cruelty but of crass ignorance.

What an ass the law is to put them on the schedule of protected birds here, with one stroke of its pen, but to allow their import and confinement with another.

36. Bill Brock turns out 'on cue'

March 21, 1969

From the moment that either of the two pilot lights flash on top of our television, the most glamorous star holds no more attractions for me than a sack of old potatoes. Party political broadcasts sink into proper perspective and protest marches are halted in their stride. Whatever programme is on the screen, we look the other way.

The entertainment we prefer is just outside our window and I described the stage management a year ago. It is played on a stage of green sward against the velvet backcloth of a starry sky. The actors are three badgers and they have the added attraction of being personal friends.

Bill Brock is the male lead and he is ably supported by two young handsome females. There is little point in trying to put up their names in lights because they are so alike that no one can tell them apart.

Bill is two years old and we got to know each other very well indeed when I reared him on the bottle. Having tried it once, I have vowed never to keep another badger in captivity. I reared Bill partly to see how long it would be before he reverted to the wild if given complete liberty and partly to find out more about the natural behaviour of badgers.

I have already described the artificial sett I built for him about a year ago (see *A dose of* melophilia). It has a long pipe tunnel as its entrance and last spring I reared two little sow cubs as companions for him.

Badgers are exceptionally clean creatures and in the wild frequently leave one sett to live for a time in another. This is not because they are not naturally 'sett trained', because they are as fastidious as old maids about their personal habits. The reason they are supposed to change setts is to avoid any chance of the bedding attracting fleas or ticks or other insects.

Our badgers are free to come and go as they please to the wood outside, so I built a second artificial sett for them near to the pool. I hoped that if they did want a change of residence they would choose this instead of digging a home for themselves perhaps on land that we didn't own.

We had taken a great deal of trouble to rear them and introduce the little sows to the old boar who might have savaged them as intruders if we had been careless. So we naturally didn't want them to wander far afield and settle in an unfriendly land where someone might have shot or gassed them or dug them out with dogs. We were also hoping to observe them far more regularly than is ever possible with wild badgers.

We were very excited when they all settled happily in the sett and began to go out naturally into the woods to feed. The snag was that we couldn't see what happened after dusk had fallen. Because they were all hand-reared, they were used to seeing the house and yard lights on so I fixed up a small floodlight to illuminate their sett.

Then we sat for hours in the evening glued to the window waiting for the first black and white face to appear at the mouth of the tunnel. It was far more comfortable than conventional badger-watching because, instead of sitting perched up in the draughty fork of an overhanging tree, we had the luxury of our own easy chairs and a crackling log fire. But our badger-watching was just as time consuming.

We had trained them as cubs to push a swinging flap to get through the fence to the wood outside. The wild foxes think this 'badger-gate' is a trap so do not follow them back to slaughter our duck.

So inside the tunnel to the sett I fitted a new swinging flap which had an electric micro-switch attached. I led a wire from the switch to the house and any badger entering or leaving the sett lights a pilot lamp on top of our television. Now we can read or talk or watch TV knowing that when the pilot light flashes we shall get all the rewards of dedicated badger watchers without their time-wasting discomfort.

The same micro-switch in the tunnel works an electro-magnet which marks a graph in my study so I am building a very comprehensive record of which periods of darkness are the busiest for badgers.

When the B.B.C. Natural History Unit heard of this experiment, they sent a camera team up for a couple of days to film our badgers. My experience of wild creatures has been that they do all sorts of exciting things when I am alone. I tell my friends who want to watch but when they come to see for themselves, nothing ever happens.

So I was very apprehensive that an expensive film crew

would arrive and Bill and his girl friends would make a fool of me and never put in an appearance.

Not a bit of it. Bill behaved as if he'd been winning Oscars all his life. He always calls at my study window before he goes off into the wood and I usually let him come into the house for a little fuss and a plate of tit-bits.

The whole side of the house was floodlit like a stage; there were strangers with whirring cameras in the study but he came in with all the confidence of an old-timer. He let the camera team follow him in daylight in the wood while he poked about for food and he behaved in general as if he did a TV feature every day of his life.

37. Mysterious migration

April 25, 1969

Even during the late cold spring there have been odd sheltered patches in the wood which have caged the most fleeting glints of sun. They are delightful spots to savour the warm promise of better things to come, and I have spent a good deal of time there lately, day dreaming of a more comfortable future.

One of the attractions of these suntraps is that their popularity is universal. A clearing at the top of the wood is used by nine fallow deer so regularly that I almost know their names. I pass within fifteen or twenty yards of them at least twice a day, with four dogs at heel, and they pay us the compliment of never bothering to get to their feet.

The air ought to be throbbing with bird song, but this year they've not had much to sing about. There is so little leaf to hide their nests that the crows eat their eggs almost before they have had time to lay them. There should be plenty of chiff-chaffs and willow warblers, and the swallows ought to have arrived by now.

I did see one willow warbler the other day, the spearpoint of his kind, which was making the most of a sheltered patch of sun. But his feathers were fluffed out and he looked as miserable as an ancient crone as he tried to kindle the embers of his life from the sun's weak rays.

There were a few redstarts in that warm spell at Easter, but I've seen no sign of them for days. Redstarts feed on insects which have normally come out of hibernation by the time they arrive, but the air is so cold and food so sparse that I fear they haven't survived.

There have been all sorts of theories of what it is that triggers off the mechanism which makes birds migrate to foreign shores. Swallows in Africa have no means of knowing what weather is like in England. They arrive on the south coast about the same date each year, so it seems fair to assume that they have some sort of built-in time clock. Or perhaps it is changing climatic conditions in Africa that suddenly impel them to leave. When our weather changes for the better, it is obvious that nesting conditions here are likely to be favourable.

It never occurred to the old-time naturalist that birds migrated at all. Remains of swallows are often found by reed cutters in the mud, so it used to be assumed that they hibernated in mud, like frogs and toads.

The real explanation eventually proved to be that flocks on migration often roosted in reed beds and, when the reeds eventually bent under their weight, they drowned in the darkness.

Then it dawned on naturalists that birds which fed mainly on insects often went to warmer climes in winter and only returned when conditions were more sympathetic. It was a revolutionary discovery and, as so often happens, obscure theories were formulated to fit it. Birds were supposed to prepare for migration, leap in the air and fly the whole way to their destination non-stop.

The pendulum has swung and it is now thought that they go by relatively easy stages. They obviously fly across the sea in one hop, and many perish if they meet head winds or are blown seriously off course.

But swallows are reported annually on the south coast several weeks before they reach Scotland. They seem to travel leisurely enough to feed off the country as they go. Perhaps they keep pace with the rising temperature as it gradually creeps from south to north.

There have been lots of theories about navigation, as well. The obvious one is that parent birds teach their off-spring where to go so that the knowledge is passed down from generation to generation. But old birds transfer their affection to the second brood, when once the first are fledged and, anyway, old and young often migrate at different seasons.

Navigation, therefore, seems to be an inherited instinct, so perhaps birds have some sort of inbuilt compass or radar? Nobody really knows, but the idea is not as far-fetched as it might sound.

Experiments have been carried out on migratory birds, which were put in an entirely closed building, with no windows to the outside world at all. The roof was domed like the sky, and stars and sun and moon were spotted-in at appropriate places where the imprisoned birds would have seen them if they had access to the outside world.

They naturally tried to escape and when they struggled, in

their impotence, they always tried to go in the direction they would have taken on migration.

To test the theory of magnetic intuition, the dome was turned through 90 degrees. Now the North star on the roof really pointed to the East. Would the birds try to migrate according to the compass or as directed by this phoney astrodome? If they went true south, they would be steering by some inborn compass, but if they followed the stars on the roof, they would be navigating by sight.

They seemed to fc'low the stars, but it wasn't as simple as that. The night sky varies from season to season and every navigator knows what sophisticated mathematics he needs to choose the correct route without a compass.

Yet the youngest and most innocent birds seem able to 'home' to the nesting place of their forefathers as accurately as a professor of aeronautics. We are not as clever as we think.

38. The heron with wriggling toes

May 2, 1969

Our herons are back on their nests, fighting their annual battles with the crows which try to steal their eggs, or spreading their wings to shield their young from treacherous showers or fitful bursts of sun.

They steal off, at first light, to snatch a few fish before fools are out with their guns. And they resume their hunt, at dusk, while the same fools are boasting in bar parlours about the quarry they almost slew.

The old birds sit hunched at the water's edge, waiting for a meal. Their monumental dejection is eloquent testimony that fishing, for them, is not sport but a dreary job of work.

Human fishermen, jealous of their skill, have formulated far fetched theories to account for their superiority. They say that the fine hairs on herons' legs are mistaken by the fish for food, or the oil exuded from their feet is an irresistible lure. One school of thought even claims that herons have only to shake the scale from their feathers, as bait on the water, for fish to swarm in from afar to their doom. Or, if they wriggle their long toes in the mud, the fish are supposed to cluster round, under the delusion that a worm is about to break surface.

We get plenty of chances to watch our herons fishing at close quarters, and I do not believe that they have found any magic charm. They owe their success to nothing but patience and the skill of sheer professionalism.

Folktales about herons are by no means confined to their prowess as fishermen. They nest in colonies and are among the noisiest and most spectacular lovers of the feathered world.

During the winter the colony disperses to aid the chance of finding food and to limit the risks of concentrating in some danger spot. The old cocks return to the colony in early spring and stake their claim to last year's nest or some coveted spot as yet unbuilt upon. There is a good deal of competitive clamour and noisy serenading to persuade the females that marriage has its charms.

At other times of the year their eyes and bills are yellow but the stimulus of love turns them fiery red in spring. This strange 'blushing' is often only transitory and is not yet properly understood. It was noted centuries ago and Aristotle in his *Historia Animalium* said that the females submitted with reluctance and that their erotic ardour made them scream till the blood dripped from their eyes.

An exaggeration perhaps but a fitting climax to a love affair which I have often watched begin as a formal dance in the pasture on the far side of our pool. About ten or a dozen birds will gather and sit hunched and hopeless as wallflowers at a village hop. Suddenly one odd bird arriving will prompt them all to rise at once and take a few steps, as if they were about to begin a Paul Jones.

They start a stately, half-hearted dance, a sort of debilitated minuet. But the first few measured treads convince them that the attractions of their partners have been overrated and they relapse, at once, into their hopeless vigil. Sometimes they give superb displays of languid aerobatics.

I watched seven last week fly off from the heronry towards Blithfield Reservoir but, half-way there, they suddenly changed their minds. What really happened, I suppose, was that eddies from the warm and steamy plough created inviting thermals. First one and then another changed direction and began to glide upwards in tight spirals.

They circled as effortlessly as buzzards, climbing ever higher on stiff outstretched wings. They shrank to sparrow size and went on climbing till, at last, they disappeared as tiny specks from sight.

More than 1,000 years B.C. the Egyptians thought that herons on this spiral flight conveyed the souls of their dead up to the gods and painted, in homage, herons on their coffins. One of the oldest folk beliefs of all has only recently been connected with herons.

At this time of year, or a little earlier, I sometimes find isolated patches of jelly in the woods. They are unpleasant, irregularly shaped lumps about the size of pocket watches. For a long time naturalists thought they were some sort of fungus and some still do, because a small lump one day, may have 'grown' the next.

Welsh shepherds call this Pydru Ser, which means the Rot of the Stars, and country folk believe that this is all that is left when a shooting star collides with Earth. It appears in such widely dispersed places, from the edge of woodland to the centre of wild moorland, that shooting stars seemed the only conceivable vehicles for such random distribution.

A more modern belief is that it is left there by herons and crows, but mostly by herons. They catch both frogs and toads but are careful not to eat the reproductive organs of the females. These organs produce the basis for the jelly of frog and toad spawn, but it only swells into the huge masses seen in pools when it comes into contact with water.

If the herons ate it neat, it would swell inside them till their indigestion was intolerable, so they wisely prepare their meal by dissecting out the waste as skilfully as the most distinguished chef.

39. Verdict by luck, not judgement

June 6, 1969

We have not been sorry to see the last petals of our blossom flutter jaded to the ground. Last autumn we ate a handful of luscious sun-warm Victoria plums every time we went into the paddock and we could stuff ourselves with damsons until we were convulsed with bellyache.

The floral crinoline of the weeping cherry on the lawn cloaked its trunk in modesty; and the crab apple trees were pinker and whiter than the complexion of the freshest country girl.

This spring promised even better things – the fact that it was exceptionally cold and wet should have delayed the blooms past the perils of late frost. They should have been even more desirable because they kept us waiting and they should have been even sweeter because there has been so little sun to scorch their innocence.

We reckoned without the bullfinches. There is always a pair nesting in the thicket up the lane or swaggering about the garden. They sit on the apple and plum trees nibbling a little blossom and spitting the confetti out on to the ground. We don't mind because we tell ourselves that it is Nature's way of thinning out superfluous fruit.

This year, though, they overdid it. Our pair must have been unusually prolific or have developed an exceptionally good bush telegraph. Bullfinches turned up in a flock and set about the blossom till the shredded petals fell like snowflakes. The lawn was pink with weeping cherry and crab apple blossom, and there were drifts under the plum and damson trees in the paddock.

The late season which we thought would cheat the frosts kept the flowers blooming so long that the bullfinches shone with health at our expense and derided us with their faint and squeaky song. They might have been shot for their pains.

Although they appear on the list of protected birds, their safety is rather precarious. Where it can be proved that they are doing damage in fruit-growing districts, the law can be amended locally to erase them from the protected schedule.

They are perfectly safe with us. My wife is a far better and keener gardener than I am, but she also has a gentler nature. Although we both agree that plenty of gardens are richer with blossom than ours not everyone can see a brilliant flock of lovely birds just outside the window.

They were wise to choose us as their victims instead of taking their chance where some owner has to earn a living the hard way by growing fruit commercially.

Luck plays an irrational part in what creatures are granted protection. If the food they eat happens to be money they are high on the danger list. Hawks, which prey on game, were almost exterminated by gamekeepers and then reprieved by the Birds Protection Acts. Then they were nearly wiped out again, this time by accident, because they preyed on creatures which were already dying of pesticide poison.

Bullfinches do a certain amount of real damage on fruit farms, so they are shot or caught in cage traps to have their necks wrung. Pigeons and starlings which foul city streets are caught and destroyed without much sympathy because they are not 'beautiful'.

The Victorians were inveterate collectors of eggs and stuffers of rarities. They even shot kingfishers to add colour to their morbid glass cases of trophies. What birds escaped the collectors in those days were likely to receive a fatal dose of lead from the gun of a gamekeeper of the old school.

Legislation was passed only just in time to prevent a great wave of extinction. But it seems odd to me that so much attention was focused on birds and so little on animals.

Wild cats and pine martens were almost wiped out and so were polecats. They were just as much part of the English countryside as falcons or kingfishers and were no more threat to human survival. Now otters have joined them on their pinnacle of peril.

One reason is that birds are far easier than animals for casual visitors to the countryside to see. They are often very beautiful and cause the most insensitive to flinch a little at the thought of their execution. I would like to see a more objective and less emotional approach to protection of our wild life.

It is possible to convince the sentimental that it is kinder to foxes to sell them as cubs for pets than it is to shoot or hunt or snare them subsequently. The fact is that the trade in young animals sometimes commits them to a most unsuitable and often miserable life sentence of imprisonment.

I know this only too well from personal experience because every season disillusioned owners of these wild animals try to foist them on to me for rehabilitation. It has been illegal for some years to cage most British birds unless they were bred in captivity. To prove it, they had to have a ring on their leg which is too small to get on after they have passed the nestling stage. I should like to see British mammals given the same sort of protection.

I should like it to be as illegal to kill an otter as a golden eagle. And I should like to see the rare ones like pine martens legally protected because they are in danger of extinction, rather than because they are 'pretty' or to prevent someone enjoying hunting them.

I should like sensible control of any hazard, be it pesticides or predators, whose numbers have swelled out of balance. Most of all I should like more sanctuaries – not for people to enjoy seeing rarities, but for rarities to have seclusion from people.

40. Roe around the house

June 13, 1969

Most zoos come fairly high on my list of pet hates. I don't like to see animals and birds confined in unnatural conditions while endless crowds file past and gawp at them. It may be true that lions and tigers pacing up and down their cages are not trying to escape. Apologists for such exhibitions claim that their automated rhythm is only an exercise pattern, but I remain unconvinced.

I was, therefore, slightly offended when an article about my tame deer produced a rude letter from a man who told me what a terrible fellow I am to keep a roe deer in captivity. I was much more worried when an eminent naturalist said that I was a fool to waste my time because roe deer were so wild and so shy and delicate that they wouldn't live long.

There are no wild roe deer in the Midlands so I knew too little about them to argue. That was seven years ago, when I was offered a tiny roe kid which had been taken to the R.S.P.C.A at Midhurst in Sussex. She is lying content outside my study window as I write, sunning herself. So much for the theory that she wouldn't live long.

If I stretched out my arm I could caress her silken ears. In theory. It would be less simple in practice because she would leap to her feet the instant she heard the window slide. Not because she was intent on escape, but so that she could come even closer and thrust her head through the window. Then she would nuzzle my hand for a piece of her favourite chocolate biscuit, which she expects every morning when I have my coffee at eleven.

The six-acre enclosure where she lives includes the pool and house and wild patches of reed and bracken and rhododendron and nut thickets. There is shade from ancient oaks and good grazing in the paddock. Just the sort of spot that wild roe deer would choose.

I put the fence round, not to cage things in so much as to give nesting duck and pheasants security from foxes. It also prevents the roe deer wandering on to farmland where they might be shot.

I say 'they' because the original kid was joined by a wild buck and doe, which were sent to me instead of being executed for ravaging crops. We feared, when we released them, that they might panic and damage themselves, but their instinct of self-preservation was wonderfully strong.

They crept into a patch of dense cover and we never caught another glimpse of them for several days till they had weighed up their situation. That doesn't mean that they were cowering in terror, not daring to move. They seem to have spent their time learning every square yard by heart so that they could put the pool between themselves and danger from whichever direction it threatened.

Then they started to come out at dawn to crop the sweet clover and, if anything alarmed them, they melted into the shadows and reappeared as if by magic on the far side of the pool.

This game of hide-and-seek, which they could always win, gave them confidence. They saw that our tame doe had nothing to fear and they soon joined her when she came to guzzle the corn we put out for the ducks.

That summer, the 'wild' doe reared a youngster in such secrecy that we saw it only about half a dozen times in the first six weeks. It is very rare indeed for roe to breed when they have not got entire freedom, but we didn't count it as 'our' success because she must have been in-kid when she arrived.

In the autumn the mother died, quite suddenly, and a post-mortem revealed that she was full of internal parasites. Perhaps my naturalist friend, who had said how difficult roe are, was right. We were naturally worried about my tame roe and the buck and kid, so the vet advised dosing them in the same way that one would worm puppies.

This entailed netting them which was a very distressing business for us as well as them. Before the second dose was necessary, we had managed to obtain a tasteless medicine which they don't seem to notice mixed with fowl corn. So now, they are dosed every three months – and they don't even know when it happens. I believe this is the key to their exceptional health.

The first kid was three years old on May 19, and about a month ago I noticed that her figure was not as trim as usual. By the last week in May, it had become obvious that she had had a kid, but there was no means of knowing whether it had survived.

Female roe visit their young only three or four times a day to suckle them. They leave them for the rest of the time lying by themselves in a thicket. The tiny creatures are only about as big as a rabbit and they are safer from their enemies lying motionless, relying on their wonderful camouflage, than if they sought safety in flight.

I was not willing to disturb them by making a systematic search so I hid and watched from a distance until the doe went to feed her kid. When she left, I crept up to examine it. It never so much as flickered an eyelid to betray its presence. Its dainty legs seemed no thicker than pencils and the white pattern on its foxy russet coat was as exquisite as the design on a fairy gown.

It was impossible to imagine how such fragility could survive in this harsh world. If it wasn't gobbled up by a predator, it must surely be washed away by the first shower of rain.

But it survived to grow into an attractive, leggy debutante. It is not shy any longer, and in the evening it follows mum right out into the open. The doe grazes quietly while the kid dances round her with the abandon of a leaf caught in a whirlwind.

One second it is under the old lady's nose, the next it is pirouetting over fallen tree trunks at the very edge of the pool.

I take it as a sign that life with us is not so bad as the man who wrote the rude letter implied.

41. Canbottle country

Foreign softwood trees on English soil never fail to vex my eyes. I dislike their regimented ranks and the sterility beneath their boughs. They may be a get-rich-quick crop, but they are a poor substitute for the spreading oaks and beech which give our native countryside such charm.

Nothing is more beautiful than English parkland, studded with ancient trees. The cattle browse the lower branches, as high as they can reach, so that they stand neat and symmetrical as giant sunshades. At sunset and sunrise they stretch dark fingers across the turf as green as only English grass can be. By high noon, the shadows have shrunk and reformed into rings of shade impregnable against the flies and heat.

Softwoods are planted like grains of corn in rows, for profit not for pride, and they kill everything green that grows below. Their resinous stink is unpalatable even to insects, so that there is nothing to attract the birds, and there is no friendly rustle of wind in leaves which can only rattle their dry spines.

But even softwoods can be charming when they are young. Before we came to Goat Lodge the woods had been divided in two and put up for sale as standing timber. Luckily the part nearest the house was still unsold, so that we were able to reprieve it and simply let it stand and grow.

The trees on the other forty acres had been sold but not felled. For months the air reverberated with the pitiless yowl of chain saws and the sickening crunch of falling timber. The licence which allowed the previous owner to cut them down stipulated that the land should be cleared and rented to the Forestry Commission for a period of 999 years. The annual rent is half a crown an acre for land which, if let to a neighbouring farmer, would have fetched at least six or seven pounds. (Sixteen or seventeen by 1974!) So it was small wonder that they can make a handsome profit.

From one point of view, it had suited us very well. Land, let for so long at such a peppercorn rent, has practically no commercial value so that we were able to acquire the additional forty acres at a price which lay within our purse.

As soon as the land was cleared, the first thing our tenants did was to plant it with tens of thousands of softwood trees. They were tiny seedlings about nine inches high and there seemed small prospect they would survive to push through the mattress of grass. For the first year or so, the foresters weeded them by walking patiently along each row, cutting the grass and bracken away from the tiny trees with razor-edged slashing hooks. This left 'furrows' with seedling Corsican pines growing in the bottom, and 'ridges' of uncut cover in between.

This was the stage in a softwood forest's life when it can be a perfect paradise for all sorts of wild creatures and for the next ten years or so even these softwood trees will be charming. The dense low herbage between the rows gives the birds security against their predators. Even the sharp-eyed crows can't find all the nests and foxes and stoats can't catch all the young.

During summer this year the air has been rich with the continuous hum of grasshopper warblers, and tree pipits have dropped from the surrounding trees, like parachutes, singing sweetly as they fell. Nightjars have started their song at dusk when other birds were silent, and the whinchats and reed buntings have sung the whole day through.

But my favourite birds of all have been the long-tailed tits. In Staffordshire, they're known as can-bottles, because they build a bottle-shaped nest of indescribable artistry. It is domed in shape, about the size of a tennis ball, with an entrance hole near to the top. It is made of moss and delicate cobwebs and its lining is formed with the softest feathers. Up to a thousand feathers have been counted by taking a disused nest apart and each has been collected singly and woven into the nest with loving care.

The birds are as dainty as the homes they build. The parents have tails as long as their bodies, with white crowns and bellies and black-and-white wings and tails. Their flanks and breasts are a most delicate pink, but this does not show on the young until they have moulted out of their juvenile plumage.

The dense cover in our young woodland suits them perfectly. They love patches of gorse and the impenetrable thicket of birch that is allowed to grow as a nurse crop for the pines.

Not surprisingly, such tiny birds, with such long ungainly tails, are rather weak in flight; their bodies are so small they easily perish in hard winter weather. Indeed, it is not uncommon to find them stiff and dead on winter mornings, frozen by their tails to the twigs where they had crept to roost.

Such fragile creatures need to have large families, of up to 10 or 12, or their species might die out. They are so sociable that two or three of these families often join to form a clan of the sweetest fairies in the wood.

In time, I fear, the pine trees will thrive at the expense of everything else. They will crowd out the undergrowth and smother the birch which nursed them. Then the foresters will bough them up so that there is nothing on the floor of the wood but a lifeless mass of tall, dry trunks.

Before that happens, I shall try to ensure continuity by making clearings in the wood by the house. I shall leave them untamed in a planned wilderness which I hope will provide a home for all the creatures which the foresters dispossess.

42. Weasels at the bottom of our garden

August 15, 1969

There is no silence so deep as silence broken by very tiny sounds. Sultry summer weather, on the edge of trees, has a background orchestration of myriads of hover flies, faint as the wood wind of musicians far away over the horizon.

Pugnacious shrew mice, screaming falsetto insults round the bramble roots, only emphasise how quiet it really is. Many gamekeepers are so well aware of this that they do their most effective work, not by heavy-booted striding round their beats, but by sitting quiet at hidden vantage points.

Few of these solitary men are enchanted by abstract beauty. Shadows lengthening into intricate patterns mean no more to them than the timetable from which they know that a fox will cross the ride to safety – if their itchy fingers do not squeeze the trigger fast enough. Their patience is rewarded as they discover that a colony of rats live in this hedgerow, a stoat in that field drain, and that hawks and owls are nesting in unsuspected places.

They know which secret bowers are the favourites of village courting couples and, though they are sometimes almost close enough to hear the thumping of their hearts, it is not the romance that interests them. What the keepers must be certain about is that love is not a subterfuge behind which a local poacher hides to learn where the pheasants roost.

This single-minded dedication eradicates every living thing which might kill a pheasant or partridge or hare, whatever other virtues it might claim. This is not so much the keepers' fault as their employers. Punitive taxation means that only the very rich can shoot for fun, or those who run their hobbies as a business.

They calculate the keeper's wage, the price of wood, the cost of rearing game and then they try to make a profit from their sport. They are predictably harsh with anything that pilfers their pickings before they ring out their worth on the poulterer's till.

Naturalists know that the strong survive at the expense of the weak in the wild, as they do in our society. It is therefore sensible to formulate a practical policy for conservation to impose a balance where some of everything can thrive. A proper proportion of predators are a positive benefit to the species on which they prey because they mop-up the weak and diseased to leave a healthy breeding stock. It is only when their numbers swell too much, as they will if left to themselves, that calculated control is necessary.

People who kill off predators indiscriminately do not know what they miss. The nest of weasels at the bottom of our garden would not last long on any decent shoot. But so far as we are concerned, they are an ornament to the place.

When they play, they chase each other round the lawn as lightly as a bunch of wind-blown leaves. Their mother, the old weasel, taught them their territory by leading them behind her as close as a chain of russet sausages. Wherever she went, they followed, the nose of each glued to his predecessor's tail. They snaked in and out of the shrubbery, played hide-and-seek in the dense thickets of the yew hedge and eventually disappeared behind the Ha-ha wall.

I tried the keeper's old dodge of 'squeaking' them out. It is easy enough by blowing on a blade of grass as country children do, or sucking one's lips in almost silent meditation. The result should be a high pitched squeak, no louder than a shrew in the bottom of a hedge. To weasels, it is as irresistible as a huntsman's horn to hounds.

Within seconds, an empty hole fills up and a snaky head, with piercing button eyes, pokes out. It would be easy not to notice her at all if the whiteness of her waistcoat didn't give the show away. That is the time when a keeper would shoot, but weasels are safe enough here.

My wife and I spent almost half an hour spellbound as the old bitch weasel hunted fieldmice in the paddock. As she weaved in and out of the tussocks, we couldn't decide whether she was hunting by ear or scent. Certainly her nose was glued like a bloodhound's to the ground but, as she drew close to her quarry, she froze in her tracks, immobile as a pointer.

She may have been taking her bearings from every fitful eddy of the breeze, but we thought she seemed to be listening. Perhaps her quarry, knowing where she was, betrayed itself by frightened breaths or noisy pulse. Whatever the signal, the hunter sized up the situation, darted into the thicket and came writhing out, united with her prey.

She dragged it off to feed her young and added three more

encores while we watched. It wasn't only mice they caught, but small birds too. And if their numbers grew so large that they had any serious effect on the small bird population, I should thin them out as surely as a keeper.

But most small woodland and garden birds have two or three broods of four or five. They are nature's contribution to the diet of her hunters. This year in the garden we have had more small birds than ever. All the nest boxes I put up have been occupied and nearly every suitable hedge and shrub and tree has made its contribution.

So the family of weasels have lived easily and well without doing any real harm. Although we do not see them as often as the birds, their sinuous grace more than compensates us when we do. Next year, I hope to build an artificial nest site for them in the bank by the sitting room window. I shall construct a long tunnel entrance, like huntsmen do for foxes, and a draught-proof kennel underground. If they take up their abode there, they will delight us as much as they would annoy a shooting man.

43. *Ghosts on Saturday night*

October 24, 1969

Our wood wears a ghostly shroud every seventh night. The other six, however bright the moon, there is nothing to see but the dense shadows of the trees faintly contrasted against the geometric patterns of the rides.

But on Saturday nights, especially when there is a wisp of mist, it is obvious that something unusual is astir. An uncanny light illuminates the silhouetted trees and is blown back as a swirling white shadow in breaths of water vapour.

Each week the light appears in a different part of the wood, and when it is near an open ride, it is clearly visible from the village a mile away and arouses natural curiosity. The first person to ask about it over a pint at the Goat's Head inn, was a perfect stranger.

I told him it was a moth trap and, apparently thinking that I had traded a silly answer for a silly question, he tipped up his pint and stalked off in high dudgeon.

Then a friend of mine came round the wood in broad daylight and noticed the stout framework, clad in steel mesh netting. He got the same answer to his question as the man in the pub, but knowing me better, he took no offence but simply remarked that our moths must be mighty tough to need a trap strong enough to hold a badger.

He was not far off target, because the stout steel cage was indeed designed to defeat the ingenuity of our badgers intent on broaching any defence against their curiosity. This cage was built, not to keep badgers in, but to keep them out.

Under a transparent lid there is a bowl, covered with a Perspex cone, crowned by an electric bulb which is lit by mercury vapour. It emits the brilliant white light which strangers mistake for a wraith floating in the tree-top mist.

Moths find it irresistible and fly straight to it through the steel mesh guard. They have huge eyes with far more facets than the most expensive diamond cut by craftsmen to sparkle in the faintest gleam.

The intricacy of insects' eyes was not created to reflect light so much as to plunder every fleeting ray and register its precise direction. This information is passed by nerves which excite the muscles on the opposite side of the body. If the illumination is brightest on the moth's right side, the muscles of the left wing will be stimulated by the light to make it vibrate faster, which automatically steers the insect towards the source of light.

It is a reflex action as inescapable as fate, and it is what causes moths to flutter round bright lights so helplessly. The moth trap in our wood was scientifically designed to exploit this weakness. When insects are lured to it by the mercury lamp, they flutter round and spiral down into the Perspex cone. Once in the trap, they find shady trays beneath which to creep for sanctuary.

It is such a ruthlessly efficient instrument that, if we left it alight every night, there would be serious danger that it might deplete the moth population of the wood. That would be the very reverse of what we want to do, so we use it with the utmost care.

My friend John Herbert who owns it, is writing a learned thesis about the population of moths which inhabit our woods. He decided that the first thing he must do is to establish precisely what species live here now, not just in the summer months, but throughout the year.

When I was a boy, the conventional way of doing this would have been to prance around, like fairies at dusk, trying to catch them in wildly waving nets. The chances of success would have been even more remote than catching butterflies by day.

Alternatively, we could have wandered round the wood, patient as shadows, seeking out the secret hiding places where insects while away the daylight hours. The snag in this is that treecreepers, and the whole host of other insectivorous birds, would be doing precisely the same thing in direct competition.

Our motive would be to advance our knowledge: theirs to satisfy their hunger. As their eyes are so much sharper than the keenest human sense, our search would have been even less exhaustive than an amateurish conquest by butterfly net.

Even in my youth, we were a bit more scientific than that. We were very fond of 'sugaring'. This entailed concocting a treacly brew of sugar, rum and water, with an aroma strong enough to incense the Excise men for miles around. Ours was no illicit whisky distillery. We used our brew to paint on trees, and called next day to collect alcoholic moths which had supped too well and passed-out on the ground below.

John Herbert's apparatus is far more efficient, and it has the advantage of leaving its captives without a thick head in the morning. I switch on the mercury light at dusk on Saturday and he comes on Sunday to count his haul. He lists them in species in his notebook and, when he has checked them, he sets them free in the deep shade of a thicket where they can be safe from predatory birds until dusk falls again.

He is going to do this each week for a year, in different parts of the wood, until his census is complete and comprehensive. When we know what is there, he will compare it with lists drawn up for the area by old-time entymologists.

Then he will compile a 'missing species' list, so that I can plant selected foods to try to attract the moths that should be here but, for some reason, have died out in the area. In days to come, I hope, we will be able to show that this moth trap has been the means of providing conditions to attract a varied population to settle here, instead of growing scarcer like the wildlife in other places.

44. Keeping the game going

November 12, 1969

No country profession has changed more than the game-keeper's. When I was a child it was rare for a keeper to be employed by anyone who did not own the land where the game was to be preserved.

Even landowners who were not shooting men usually employed gamekeepers and included the cost of their wages in the rent of any sporting rights let over their property.

This is still a sensible precaution because it prevents greedy tenants over-shooting and spoiling the long-term potential by ensuring that the keeper's loyalties are to the man who owns the land.

I spent a good deal of time as a boy in the company of keepers who worked for an impoverished landowner. The estate was reputed to be heavily mortgaged and the huge house was presided over by an ancient, cadaverous butler in a shiny suit which started life black but was by then rich green with age.

The Squire's clothes were equally shabby country tweeds and his car was an ancient banger – but he still employed five keepers. Each keeper looked after about 500 acres and his main duties were to discourage poachers and vermin. It was a mining district and the poachers had mostly roamed all over the estate bird nesting when they were children and they had paid for being caught with a hiding from an ash plant which would get a modern keeper six months in gaol for assault.

By the time they were old enough to poach they could give most wild foxes a start at getting under cover, and they knew just which bolt holt to take if they were pursued. The hardships of working underground made them pretty rough handfuls. If the keeper did manage to corner them, though, it was a point of honour with both sides to fight clean.

Nowadays most poaching is done with rifles by sneak thieves in cars and they are as likely as not to slip a knife or put a boot into anyone who opposes them.

The old-fashioned keeper spent most of his time catching vermin. To him, vermin was anything that could kill a pheasant or partridge at any stage after it came into the world as an egg. Stoats, weasels, rats, cats, crows, magpies, hawks and owls all ended up on the keeper's gallows tree.

The only exceptions among predators were foxes and dogs, which were decently buried out of sight for the simple reason that, in the keeper's view, hunting men and pet owners were prone to be a little narrow-minded.

Vermin killing has also changed since then. Gintraps are illegal and many predatory birds are now on the protected list and spared. Indeed, I know one keeper who is proud of the fact that two pairs of sparrow hawks nest on 'his' estate though he would have been sacked for it twenty-five years ago. It is now also quite common to find keepers in naturalist societies, where their practical knowledge is highly regarded.

But the biggest change is on the rearing field in spring. I can remember a team of horses pulling an old shepherd's hut on wheels – a sort of miniature caravan – to a different field each year. Fresh ground was chosen to avoid disease being carried over from one year's birds to the next. Eggs were produced by catching-up pheasants that had survived the shooting season and caging them in fox-proof runs. Then rows and rows of hen coops were put out along the edge of the rearing field with a broody hen to incubate each clutch of eggs.

The keeper never slept at home from April until his birds went into cover in late summer, but literally lived on the rearing field in his little mobile hut. He surrounded the area, like a minefield, with greedy gintraps and he was out with his gun from dawn to dusk, annihilating any predator foolish enough to come within range.

He had more secret recipes than an arch-witch for concoctions of rice and shredded rabbit and greenstuff and corn, which he brewed-up in a pig-swill boiler in a corner of the field. I often thought that the pheasant poults fed better than the Squire.

For all this devotion, the keeper received less than £1 a week, and a cottage when he had time to enjoy such luxury. Now, keepers are paid at least as much as agricultural workers, and usually much more. They have modern cottages and a field car to get quickly from one side of the beat to the other, or to take the children to school.

Walkie-talkie radios help outwit poachers, eggs are hatched in incubators by the thousand, and poults are reared in vermin-proof runs. Instead of walking miles a day, scattering grain which wild birds usually found before the pheasants, modern keepers have devised self-feed hoppers as simple as cafeteria. They fill a tin with grain and cut slots through which the pheasants can help themselves as they want.

Unfortunately, the wood pigeons find them too and while modern keepers are sitting at home watching the telly, their grain stores are raided by uninvited guests.

The feeding hoppers and electronically-controlled incubators, mechanical transport and radio-controlled communications are all symptoms of this change from art to science in the keeper's life.

45. Who cares about the countryside?

December 5, 1969

The green heart of England is being eaten out by hordes of planners and developers, road builders and reservoir diggers. The exploding population will continue to demand more and more food, more water, more space for recreation, and acres of fertile land for every mile of motorway.

Nothing short of war or plague or massive use of birth control can halt the demand and it is all too easy to become emotional about the implications. It is easy to bemoan the loss of fair countryside that we should hold in trust for future generations.

It is just as tempting for the other side to ask what a few wild birds or rare plants or threatened insects matter when the welfare of people is at stake. It is the politicians who are in final control of what is done and they depend for their power on our votes.

It so happens that the conflicting interests of development, for profit, and food production and exploitation of leisure, are not entirely incompatible with the aspirations of the conservationists. There could be room for both and it should be possible to devise a plan so that some areas are spared for wildlife and amenity. Conservation should mean the management of land for the benefit of as wide a variety of interests as possible.

Although it is true that wild birds do not vote, a civilised, as opposed to permissive, society ought to be able to find it possible to provide living space for creatures whose ancestors were here when our forefathers were running round in skins and woad.

The crux of the problem is votes. If enough people care about conserving our wildlife, the planners and politicians will bow to their wishes. If those who mind are an insignificant minority, there will soon be no wild place left to mind about.

Christopher Fuller is a young man who appreciated the importance of this fact some years ago. He realised that before he could make much impact, it was first necessary to discover how many urban people, who hold the majority of votes, understood or cared about wildlife conservation.

Between November 1964 and September 1965 while working in Bristol, he organised a survey in the city to test the views of a large urban population on wildlife conservation. He later joined the Nature Conservancy and this year repeated the survey, once more entirely independently, but this time in the smaller town of Shrewsbury. He published both surveys under the title *An Urban Survey of Views on Wildlife Conservation.*

The first question he asked was 'Are you interested in any aspect of (a) animal life or (b) plant life, in its natural surroundings?'

In Bristol, with the larger population, 66 per cent of the people asked were interested and in Shrewsbury 70 per cent. Only 17 per cent and 18 per cent respectively were not interested in either. In spite of the 17 per cent who were not personally interested, only four of the total of 322 people (little more than 1 per cent) thought that conservation of plant and animal life was unimportant.

One difference between these surveys and many public opinion polls was that they were carried out in the homes of people being questioned so that there was an opportunity to get views in greater depth than from the usual Yes-No answers.

They were asked if they thought that wildlife was adversely affected by large-scale buildings, and development, intensive agricultural methods, pesticides, drainage of marshland, reservoir and dam construction, hunting and shooting for sport, and large-scale poaching. There was substantial agreement in both towns about most of these factors.

The worst offender was thought to be pesticides, and the least damage was attributed to reservoir construction and drainage of marshland. Large-scale poaching was thought to be damaging by 93 per cent of the people in Bristol and 84 per cent in Shrewsbury, which surprised me because nothing in the questions so far had indicated that the discussion was worldwide and, had I been asked, I should have assumed that it was confined to this country.

While I agree that the poaching of animals for women's furs and zoos can be very harmful, I do not believe that poaching is a serious factor in this country if only because we are becoming too effete to be skilled at such a primitive art.

The differences between Bristol, a large city, and Shrewsbury, a country town, threw an interesting sidelight on the differences between urban and rural attitudes to hunting and shooting for sport, and on intensive farming.

In Bristol, 74 per cent thought intensive agricultural methods harmful but in Shrewsbury only 64 per cent. In Bristol, 83 per cent thought hunting and shooting for sport harmful, but only 55 per cent in Shrewsbury.

Having established that a high percentage of the people in both areas were aware of the dangers, the survey went on to examine how much people knew about organisations set up to preserve wildlife. It is again significant that more people in big cities knew about such bodies than in the smaller towns. The only exception was that more people in Shrewsbury knew about the Nature Conservancy, though that may well have been because the Midlands headquarters is on their doorstep at Attingham.

Only about half the people interviewed said that they would be willing to give active help, even with more and better publicity. But 90 per cent were willing to dip into their pockets, though not too deeply, to give financial support.

By far the most depressing answer was that only seven out of the total 322 people questioned – about 2 per cent – actually belonged to any organisation devoted to conservation. Yet almost 70 per cent of the same people thought that planning and development bodies did not take enough notice of advice from the very organisations they failed to support.

We get what we are prepared to put up with and it is useless to grumble about our vanishing wild places if we are not willing to do something constructive about it.

Everyone who cares should join his local naturalist trust. There is one in every county; the subscription will be only about £1 a year and will be mainly used to buy threatened sites to make wildlife reserves. And his support will be used to swell the number of votes to more than the miserable 2 per cent that this survey indicates as the only people willing to do anything better than grumble.

46. Informers in feathers

December 19, 1969

It is almost impossible to set foot in our wood without being showered by a noisy string of abuse by an old jay from the safety of a thicket. If I were a gamekeeper, I would probably shoot him because jays prey on eggs and nestlings, and there are no more obvious eggs or defenceless nestlings than pheasants on a well-keepered shoot.

A few pairs of jays can do irreparable damage in April and May, not only to game birds, but to even more vulnerable songbirds, but I still enjoy their company in moderation. I only thin them out if their population swells too much.

It is perfectly true that they do raid the early nests, but they also weed out the weakly, which might have infected the strong with disease if left to die of natural causes. They also rank high among our most beautiful birds. Their pink feathers would do credit to a maiden's blush, if that is not an anachronism, and the gaudy blue patches on their wings add a touch of gaiety to the most sombre winter day.

I confess to a sneaking admiration for such rascals who are always so eager to cock a snook at Authority. The more intelligent keepers suffer a few jays, not out of admiration for their aesthetic beauty, but for far more practical reasons. Jays are inveterate scolds, with eyes as sharp as village gossips. Nothing stirs in the wood that they do not spot and they cannot resist telling the world what they've seen.

So good keepers cock their ears for the chatter of the jays, because it will lead them to weasels, rats, hawks, owls, cats and poachers. They find it worth sparing one villain if he informs about so many others.

I can walk quietly all day without seeing more than a fraction of the other creatures which are sharing the countryside with me. So I stop now and again, and sit motionless on a fallen trunk or lean against a gate and listen.

The jay, which is insulting something half a mile away, may be coming nearer and I know that, if I discipline myself to immobility, I have only to wait to see a fox or a stoat which I

143

should never have noticed if the jay had not made such a song about its presence.

Sometimes I play a game of stalk the stalker. Every time the jay is busy chattering, I sneak a few yards in his direction. When he is silent and, therefore, not concentrating on his victim, I stay still too. Success at this game unfolds all sorts of dramas which would otherwise have been played out, unseen, backstage.

But it is no use pretending that the weapon is not double-edged. The chattering of a jay can tell a poacher where the keeper is as easily as it can warn a keeper of the approach of a poacher. There are tricks in every trade and the jays hold no monopoly of clues if it is possible to glean about what to look for.

Although I spent a lot of my youth with keepers, I learned even more from poachers, and the most skilful poacher I know can still catch more pheasants by night than a shooting party does by day. This man taught me about the calls of birds which are not the songs described in the bird books!

Blackbirds chatter to warn of cats or owls or people, and an ear even as unmusical as mine, can easily tell the difference in the warnings. There is not only a change in the depth of note, from a harsh metallic chatter to a sound as mellow as water dripping into deep pools, but the frequency alters. With practice, it is possible to forecast whether a fox or an owl or a keeper will appear — and to have taken evasive action by the time he does.

Silent warnings are often just as effective. We do not keep a cat because of the damage he would do to the birds, but I have often noticed that a cat by the fire will turn his head and twitch his ears, at the approach of a stranger, long before the sharpest house dog has sensed that there is anything amiss.

Of course cats, being the selfish idlers they are, could not care less if a burglar did come so long as he did not disturb them. So if you do not take the hint of their twitching ears, you have nobody to blame but yourself.

Our roe deer are just as effective, for they stop grazing and lift their heads long before the dogs have noticed an intruder's approach.

Last week, I was watching an old hare at her toilet just as it was getting light. She had obviously fed well during the night and was content. She began by licking the grains of soil from the harsh fur on her pads. When this stiff hair was dry and clean, she used it as a combined brush and comb to rub her ears until they shone like silk and to brush the dew drops out of the fur of her coat.

She was sitting about thirty yards from the wood on the short grass of my neighbour's field, as obvious for all to see as a molehill. Then, with no warning at all, she suddenly disappeared as if the ground had swallowed her up. She had 'clapped', or crouched so flat that, if I had not known precisely where she was, I should never have spotted her.

Every countryman knows that if you see a hare in a field which stays the same size as you get nearer to it, it is not a hare but a clod of soil. Only if it gets smaller is it a hare.

The hare I was watching got smaller all right but I knew it was not because she had seen me. So I stayed still and waited. Within seconds, an old fox came out of the wood and trotted across the field without either seeing or smelling her. She did not panic into dangerous flight, but coolly let the peril pass and, as soon as it was safe, resumed her fastidious toilet.

She was proof that the best watchdogs do not always have the loudest barks!

47. *Deer Sugar Daddy*

January 2, 1970

The sinister-looking character raiding our bird table is neither a four-footed pirate nor a mythical unicorn. He is our roe buck, caught in what, for such a handsome fellow, must be a most embarrassing state of undress.

About the turn of every year, his antlers fall off, and, within a few days, he deteriorates from extrovert virility into a pathetic creature who could easily be mistaken for one of his wives.

Deer grow a fresh set of antlers every year and, when they have served their purpose, some of the bone at the base of the antler is re-absorbed by the skull. This makes the joint so fragile that the least tap will cause the whole antler to fall off. This process of embrittlement is so sophisticated that both antlers are ready to fall almost simultaneously. This season our buck had both antlers intact one day, one the next and none the following morning. He looked very lopsided on the middle day!

Within a few hours, the solitary antler had gone and his head was bare and smooth. This did not last long. Within a week, two tiny buttons appeared on his skull and I am now watching them growing day by day. When fourteen weeks have passed, I shall hope to see a resplendent pair of antlers, even better than the last.

During the whole of this time, they will not be horny weapons of masculine offence, but so tender that the least tap would make their owner wince, whilst the slightest damage might cause serious malformation.

Antlers could not grow so fast if they were solid bone, so they are formed of living tissue with hot blood coursing through it. They have a covering sheath of hair of the texture of finest velvet. By April my buck will look superb but, so long as he is 'in velvet', he will take as great care of himself as the most effeminate dandy. Then the coronets, or swellings, at the base of his skull, where the antlers join it, will constrict and harden and cut off the blood supply.

This seems to produce an intolerable itch which makes him scratch, tentatively at first, in case it hurts, against sapling trees about as thick as a man's thumb. When he discovers that the antlers themselves have hardened off, leaving nothing alive but the velvet, he thrashes his head about more and more vigorously.

He wanders endlessly round the edge of his territory, growing more and more excited as the velvet is ripped into bloody shreds, which are scuffed off by the rough bark of the trees as he frays against them. Not only does he fray off his antlers, he frays the bark off the trees as well. This is what makes deer more unpopular with foresters than any damage they do by eating shoots or leaves.

He goes on fraying till every shred of velvet is destroyed, leaving the antlers clean and burnished as the blade of a sword. Even this does not satisfy him because although there are no wild roe deer within many miles of us, he takes no chances of rivals muscling-in on his preserve.

Round and round he goes, thrashing nut bushes, young oaks and birches. This is partly to work up his paddy in case another buck does appear, and partly to get the whole area reeking of his scent to warn interlopers what to expect if they do come. He is in prime condition – and the foulest temper – in time for the rut in July, when the does are ready to mate.

The seasons when deer cast their antlers vary with different species. In Red deer, the biggest of all in this country, the stags cast in March and are usually clean of their velvet in July. Fallow deer, which run wild in our wood, cast in May and are mature and clean again by August, in plenty of time for an October rut.

Antlers are not weapons of defence against predators, or does would be armed with them. They are weapons of offence, with which some rival males can procure for themselves the maximum number of females. Not that their battles are often to the death. They normally lock antlers and push like rugby forwards, till one is shoved off its feet, or weakens and tries to break away.

This is the instant of peril. The winner tries to drive his antler into the flank of his adversary as he turns away while the vanquished tries to dodge punishment by flight.

There are two snags about annual changes of antlers which are not immediately obvious. The first is that a substance so solid and bony takes an enormous amount of calcium and phosphate to build it up, and these salts are only normally obtainable in minute doses from the plants on which the deer feed. So deer have an almost insatiable craving for these mineral salts, which can be satisfied to some extent in the wild by eating cast-off antlers as they fall to re-absorb their mineral salts.

I help our deer, both the tame roe and the wild fallow, by putting out mineral 'licks' which are basically blocks of pure rock salt with traces of other minerals added.

The great prehistoric deer, whose fossilised remains are sometimes excavated, had such enormous antlers that some scientists believe that they became extinct largely because the annual drain on their vitality debilitated them so badly.

The other snag is that antlers are a visible barometer of virility. As a buck grows, his head develops in magnificence until he reaches his prime. Rival bucks are warned that here is a power to be reckoned with, and eligible does take notice, and are anxious to fall under his spell.

But, when his prime is past and his powers wane, his antlers grow less impressive year by year, until it becomes brutally obvious that, whatever conquests he may have made in the past, he is now only fit to become the deer equivalent of a sugar daddy.

48. Icy dusk

I know few sights more lovely than the wild duck silhouetted on our frozen pool at twilight. The grey trees are etched stark against the sky and the wintry sunset picks them out in rosy hues.

The water at this time of year hovers critically around freezing point. The slightest catch of frost will skin it over, but the moment the thaw comes there is a fresh flow of water from the woods. It gushes in so fast that it often floods the surface of the ice, polishing it into a mirror which doubles the duck population.

It is this which makes dusk our favourite time of day. We are not ruled by the clock and I do not return to the house at any specific hour. I come in, often cold and wet, as soon as the light begins to fade and my wife and I drink our tea by the log fire and let evening creep up on us from outside.

Great flocks of crows congregate from miles around and we watch them going to roost in the wood until their blackness merges with the sky. Even when it grows too dark to see them, we can hear the stragglers calling to their fellows to check that all is safe.

Quite often a fox comes out before the sun goes down and sits and scratches in the ride. He is obviously itchy after the day in his frowsty den and performs a leisurely toilet before setting out to catch his food.

Hares graze in the pasture and the pheasants are crowing, but when the pool is frozen it is the beauty of the duck which fills our eyes and we are anxious to see what strangers join them. We reckon that about thirty are ours. They are free to come and go as they like, but this nucleus stays here all the year and nests in the paddock and shrubbery.

They are mostly mallard, descended from ducklings I reared under a broody bantam when we came six years ago. Now they are as tame as the duck in city parks. Their faith must be infectious because the truly wild duck flying over realise that there must not only be food here but security as well.

The first time these strangers call it is nearly always dusk or dawn. They try to spend the day at the centre of large sheets of water, well out of range of men with guns. Then, as the light begins to fade, they fly off to graze for the grains of corn spilt on stubble or to forage in small pools for the weed or insects which thrive there.

Their sensitive ears pick up the faintest sounds of contented quacking and they fly cautiously down to prospect any likely feeding sites. The instant they spot our well-fed flock, they break off their flight-lines to circle the pool.

We see them first high up as small black stars against the leaden sky, often twenty or thirty together, bunched like racing pigeons. Then two or three will peel out of the formation to come in lower, still circling, with sharp eyes probing for ambushed danger.

This is a wise precaution. Blithfield reservoir, two miles from us as the duck flies, is one of the best wintering grounds for wild duck in the country. Mixed flocks of several thousands often spend their days in safety there. Shooting men know this and bait the local ponds with barley by the bucketful. They build hides of straw bales or corrugated sheets or use bushes already growing there and wait to shoot the birds which come down to feed.

The difference between these local pools and ours – apart from the fact that we don't shoot the duck – is that there are no resident flocks on other pools. They would all disappear at the first crack of gunfire.

When the wild birds circle high over us, two or three scouts come lower in to see if it is really as safe as it seems. As soon as they are satisfied, they land to join our feeding birds and their fellows come down from above and break off in groups to join them.

We never grow tired of watching the ever changing patterns as they splash down into the water, and the reflections of their continuous movement are a constant joy. We amuse ourselves counting how many accept our invitation to supper. Just before the last spell of hard winter, we notched up a total of ninety-six.

When the pool froze over, the visitors forsook us for the running water of unfrozen rivers, leaving our resident flock to swim round and keep a patch of open water for themselves.

I have never been a glutton for rarities and am just as happy to see our gorgeous-hued mallard – however common they are – as I am when some notability arrives. But I do take it as a compliment when some of the shyer species take courage from our brazen birds and venture close up to the window to feed with them.

Last week there was a beautiful pintail drake feeding by the house and a party of widgeon were calling to each other on the pool. As we fell asleep, we could hear their whistles floating in through the open bedroom window.

Soon, perhaps in another five or six weeks, we shall have parties of teal, the tiniest British ducks, feeding with the others in the open paddock. They are among the prettiest, and certainly among the shyest of our birds, and when I see how wonderfully a little security tames them, it does seem sad to torment them so with barrages of gunfire.

49. *Hounding the foxhunters*

January 30, 1970

Contrary to popular belief, fox hunting is not much more than two centuries old. Before that, when the land was mainly wood with fringes of farmland round the villages, most packs of hounds were harriers and hares were their quarry.

Fox hunting really came into its own between 1650 and 1750, in the heyday of the great estates owned by noblemen who let their land to tenant farmers. Owners of these stately homes often kept a pack of hounds to amuse themselves and their friends, and they hunted the country bounded by their own estates.

In those days an offer to pay a subscription towards the upkeep of hounds would have been taken as a personal insult. Landowners had not yet been crippled by taxation and they thought no more about keeping a pack of hounds than they did of having adequate servants or gamekeepers.

Because packs were private, Masters could control precisely who followed. The field usually consisted of the aristocracy and their friends, their doctors, lawyers, parsons and tenant farmers. By our standards, perhaps they were rather a snobby lot, but among themselves, they had the bond of common interest.

By the end of the 1914–18 war, taxation had made subscription packs fairly common. Hounds, hunt servants and their horses began to cost one man less because the rest of the followers chipped-in to pay expenses. The price of their subscription bought them the right to follow hounds.

My father-in-law was a keen hunting man before the Great War and his greatest pride was being first up to hounds. For such men it was a sort of steeplechase, over an uncharted course, and every horse which refused or rival who bit the dust gave them satisfaction.

It was a highly competitive sport and they did not give a damn whether the fox escaped or was killed so long as they were up at the front when it happened.

Between the wars farming was in the doldrums and taxation was high so the great estates broke up. Some farmers who did not go broke did well enough to buy their farms cheap and other land was snapped up by businessmen or financiers who called in mortgages at critical times. The countryside became a patchwork of small parcels owned by a multitude of individuals instead of huge blocks in the hands of a few great landowners.

It became necessary – in theory – to obtain permission of hundreds instead of dozens of people to gallop across their land. But tradition in the countryside dies hard. There are still about two hundred packs of hounds and they still hunt the country by tradition that they hunted by right when the landowners were in power.

If you want to shoot or fish you have to own or rent the sporting rights, but you still hunt across land owned by complete strangers unless they specifically forbid you.

Two things are altering this. Shooting men and the motor car. The cost of preserving pheasants is high and shooting men often live far enough away from their preserves to ignore local opinion and forbid hounds in their coverts. It is illegal to cross a motorway on horseback and dangerous to allow hounds to hunt on any major road.

This means that large parts of the country may suddenly become forbidden land. It is also impossible to ride through large areas of unbroken woodland – and the Forestry Commission plantations are expanding inexorably.

One Midland pack which is suffering from these effects is the South Staffordshire Hunt. Cannock Chase has grown up since the 1920s until it is useless for hunting and the M6 has sterilised another huge slab. They borrowed some land east of the Trent from the Meynell Hunt but now the Meynell too are suffering from new roads and they need the country back. If they take it, and it seems likely that they will, this could be the last season of the South Staffs as an independent hunt. They and the Meynell might join for the sake of combining the two countries.

In the olden days, hounds were either hunted by professionals or by amateurs who ate, drank, waked and slept hounds. Their minds were so one-track that they seemed to think like foxes and were completely in tune with the job. Now many packs are hunted by businessmen who claim the privilege because they put most money in the kitty.

I had the experience of dining with three masters of hounds and asked them to tell me what motive most of their followers had. Few were interested in watching hounds work and fewer understood the science of hunting. Contrary to popular belief, they did not go to see a kill, because there are now so many followers that they need a field master to marshal them and they often do not catch up with hounds till all is over.

The consensus of opinion was that 'they go for a damn good gallop'. If that is really so, they could have a good gallop after bloodhounds hunting a man who was briefed to keep off farmland, away from roads and out of pheasant coverts.

I watched bloodhounds hunt the stonewall country on the moors above Buxton and, judging by the falls I saw, it not only took a brave man to follow them, but a skilful one too.

Perhaps there is not the thrill of quarry on an unknown line, but soon I think there will be no choice. It won't be the anti-bloodsport societies that will put an end to hunting. It will be the pressure of the motor car and mechanical farming.

50. My badger's love life

February 13, 1970

My fingers are crossed in the hopes of better luck this spring than I had with my badgers last year. I then had two yearling sow badgers and my old boar, Bill, who was a year older. I had reared them all on the bottle and persuaded them to settle in an artificial sett in sight of the sitting room window.

They were perfectly free to come and go to the unfettered wood outside, but I put out a nightly dish of bread-and-treacle to encourage them to return to sleep in safety here during the day.

My ambition was to make them so much at home that they would breed in the sett I had built and give me the chance to study a litter of growing cubs under natural conditions, at closer quarters and more continuously than anyone had done before. Although badgers are relatively common, surprisingly little is known about them. It is not even known if they are monogamous and pair for life, or whether the master boar of a colony collects for himself a harem of two or more sows. It is even possible that badgers are promiscuous.

Female badgers do not breed in their first season and before they came into breeding condition one of mine failed to return from the wood. So I am no wiser whether or not they are monogamous, because there was no chance for Bill to prove the point by kicking one of them out of the sett.

At first I thought that my sow was missing because she had found more attractive conditions than I could provide, but this comforting thought was soon knocked on the head. I was told that five badgers had been caught locally in snares within a few weeks and that some of them appeared to have come from my direction. There is nothing illegal about snaring badgers so that I could do nothing about it.

Many farmers believe that badgers kill lambs, and whatever arguments I have produced in the past I have never convinced them otherwise. In my own mind, I believe that they do not kill lambs (except the exceptional old and decrepit rogue badger, and even that has never been proved) and I believe that the culprits are almost always dogs or foxes.

In any case, it is almost impossible to set snares which will catch foxes, but not badgers, so that this time of year is exceptionally dangerous for either foxes or badgers to wander near any field where sheep are kept for lambing.

The fact that my little sow failed to return this time last year was merely circumstantial evidence that she probably came to a sticky end.

Her sister has always been a bit of a gad-about and has often been missing when respectable badgers should be safely at home. She stayed out on June 29 last year and didn't return home until July 28. The evenings were light then and my wife and I often saw her when we were wandering in the woods towards dusk. We knew it was her because she came up to within about five yards when wild badgers would, of course, have run away. But she always accompanied us, taking no notice of the dogs, which also pointed to the likelihood of it being our badger.

This period when she was missing was very important because July is the main badger rut, or mating season, and we twice saw her accompanied by a wild badger.

She came home for only three days between October 6 and November 15, which was also very significant because, if she was not successfully mated in July, she would come in season again in November.

Badgers have a most peculiar breeding cycle because, whether they are mated in July or November, makes no difference to the time they have their cubs. They normally have cubs in late February or March. This is caused by a phenomenon known as delayed implantation. The egg cell, fertilised at mating in either July or November, stays about the size of a pinhead till the end of the year. Only then does it attach itself to the wall of the uterus so that normal gestation can occur. It is even said that if badgers are subjected to exceptional shock, it is possible for the egg cell to remain unattached till next season.

There is as yet no proof of this, but it has been reported that wild female badgers, caged completely alone, have produced young more than a year after capture.

So I am waiting anxiously to see if my remaining sow has cubs this year. I scrutinise her silhouette with the anticipation of a doting mother whose daughter has married an earl, but so far I have been unable to convince myself that her figure is other than maidenly. If she does prove in cub, I fear that Bill is not the father, though she still shares the sett with him as brazenly as if she never spent a night away from home.

To limit her chances of painful strangulation in a steel wire fox-hang, I have bolted the trapdoor which lets the badgers into the wood outside. So she and Bill are temporarily caged within the six acre enclosure which keeps the ducks safe from foxes and the deer safe from foxhounds.

I dislike caging them in even though they have so much space to roam, and I will free them again when the lambs are grown and there is less chance of every hedgerow being festooned with cunning wire nooses.

The B.B.C. have fitted the sett with a permanent microphone so that, if she does have cubs, I can make recordings of the whole range of badger vocabulary over twelve months. Otherwise I shall have to possess myself in patience for yet another year in the hope that she will be more obliging next season.

51. Sanctuary for deer

February 20, 1970

A film about deer to be shown on television next week will include the herd of Pere David's deer at Woburn which would have been extinct, but for the vision of the late Duke of Bedford. He was a naturalist far ahead of his time.

It illustrates the economic possibilities which Charles Lucas is exploiting with his red deer at Warnham Park. And it highlights some of the problems which lie ahead because of human pressure on wild herds, like the fallow deer on Cannock Chase.

The Pere David's deer, at Woburn, were discovered by a French priest in 1860 in the Honan district of China. No European ever saw them entirely wild because they were kept in the Imperial Hunting Park near Peking. The Emperor and his friends were more interested in their sport than in any aesthetic qualities of these beautiful deer. So long as they were used for sport, however, they were carefully preserved.

Then in 1894, the Hun-Lo river flooded and breached the wall of the Imperial Hunting Park, allowing the deer to escape. Their freedom was short lived because the herd was speedily hacked to pieces by hordes of hungry Chinese.

The Duke of Bedford heard of the tragedy and managed to rescue a pair which he put in his park at Woburn. The original stock in China were harried to extinction but these Woburn deer flourished until there is now a strong herd, from which most of the world's zoos have been stocked. So the danger of extinction has evaporated.

At about the time the Duke of Bedford was saving Pere David's deer, a red stag was being hunted near Horsham in Sussex. It was not a wild deer but a carted stag, which had been released in front of hounds. The custom was, when hounds eventually brought it to bay, not to kill it but to catch it up and cart it back to hunt another day.

This stag was lucky because it happened to jump the fence into Warnham deerpark and Mr Lucas, the owner, refused to catch it up because he did not want his herd of fallow deer disturbed. The escaped stag settled down and grew a fine pair of antlers and the new owner was so delighted that he bought a harem of hinds to run with it.

They formed a herd of such exceptional quality that they became world-famous and the present owner, Mr Charles Lucas, showed them to me with the greatest pride. They run free in his park and, far from being an expense, they earn him more money than he could wrest from the land by conventional agricultural enterprise.

He keeps their pedigrees as if they were prize cattle, breeds them selectively to improve their quality and culls out those which do not match up to his standards. His stags regularly fetch up to £500 or £600 apiece, and they leave the imprint of their old ancestor who escaped from hounds last century.

The third – and major – part of Tuesday's film deals with the wild fallow deer of Cannock Chase. This herd was chosen for two reasons. It is a herd which is especially vulnerable to human disturbance, and it is managed by the man who is acknowledged to be a national expert on fallow deer.

Gerald Springthorpe, the Forestry Commission deer warden who includes Cannock Chase in the area he manages, last year received the Vincent Balfour-Browne award. This goes to the man who is judged to have done more than anyone else in the country for the conservation of fallow deer. On Saturday, February 28th, he goes to London to pass his award on to Mr Peter Garthwaite, who has been responsible for the welfare of all wildlife on Forestry Commission lands in this country.

The film taken on Cannock Chase shows what can be done by the proper management of wild deer. Much of it was shot from the large observation hide which was erected by the Commission and can now be hired by members of the public who want to watch deer in their natural surroundings. It shows precisely what anyone sitting quiet up there can see for himself.

The secret of success with these Cannock Chase deer is that Gerald Springthorpe has improved the quality and quantity of feed in the areas farthest from public roads and farmland. He has sown the rides and firebreaks with various mixtures of seeds to discover what deer will thrive on best. In hard weather, friendly farmers give him waste potatoes and hay the cattle could not eat.

The worst problem is disturbance by the public and their dogs. The deer flee across the roads and many are killed by traffic when they are returning. Some are driven on to the farm-land, where they are shot.

These hazards are much worse on the open part of the Chase, administered by Staffordshire County Council, and they are very lucky to have such a knowledgeable neighbour to call on for advice.

The real need for the future is to choose areas which are traditionally favourites of deer and to create inviolate sanc-tuaries there, free from public disturbance.

52. *Birth control by accident*

February 27, 1970

I sometimes wonder how much good such worthy projects as European Conservation Year really do. Most of us are already alive to the need to limit pollution of air and rivers, and to conserve wildlife while there is still some wildlife to conserve. But the conservationists pour out their jargon so incessantly that there is a temptation to write it off as political clap-trap.

The whole effort is in danger of degenerating into a series of dry academic symposia and conferences where the only audience the erudite lecturers can muster, are the equally erudite conservationists, who are already converted to their cause.

It is not necessary to attend conferences to appreciate what stupid things are commonly done in the country in the guise of scientific advancement. Perhaps it is sometimes inevitable that wildlife should be put at risk by the chemicals intended only for pests. But the risks do not always end with wildlife.

A few days ago, a story which originated in the technical medical Press painted the other side of the picture.

A number of farmworkers discovered that they had suddenly become impotent and it took doctors varying times, from weeks to months, to restore them. The precise cause of their trouble was not disclosed, but they had all been handling chemicals used on the land and those most exposed took longest to recover.

It was emphasised that the sprays in question had been clearly labelled with instructions about the precautions it was necessary to take. If this advice had been scrupulously followed, the men might well have suffered no ill effects.

But the instructions did not tell the wild animals and birds to keep off the land which had been treated. There was nothing to stop them eating the same contaminated matter which had needed no more than casual contact to render human beings impotent.

Learned lectures are not needed to teach us the lesson which was known to every simple coal miner of my youth. Mining villages in those days were famous for their aviaries of canaries.

Slim Yorkshire canaries were kept for their good looks and they had the sexless elegance of willowy fashion models. I preferred the rollicking melody of the roller canaries, which were more popular in the Midlands.

It did not make much difference whether they were kept for their beauty or their song. Their practical purpose was to test atmospheric purity and they were lowered down the pit in cages before the miners descended. The smallest concentration of gas made them roll off their perches long before dull human senses realised the air was not fit to breathe.

Naturalists have realised for years the serious danger of poison that scientists put on the land. One example has been the decline in population of some of our birds of prey. Sparrow hawks have decreased dramatically but not because they ate the crops treated with modern insecticide. It is far more insidious than that.

Insects ate the poison and birds ate the poisoned insects. When the birds became ill, they became the easiest prey for the hawks to catch. The result was that sparrow hawks ate an abnormally high proportion of birds which had been feeding on poisoned insects. The concentration of poison was often too low to kill the hawk, but still high enough to make it sterile.

Naturalists raised a hullabaloo, but the politicians simply said that increased food production was more important than the fate of a few wild birds. There was also a great deal of money to be made by the chemical industry. They would have been wiser to regard wild birds in the same light that the miners of my youth regarded their canaries.

They were sharp enough to read the clue when their birds indicated that the air in the pit was not safe to breathe. They rescued their birds and took steps to remedy the danger.

There is a similar lesson to be learned from the fate of our wildlife. If minute doses of insecticides can destroy the fertility of sparrow hawks, it is logical to fear for human beings who become severely contaminated. The farm labourers who recently figured in the medical Press might well agree – and so might others suffering from the same complaint, but have not yet diagnosed the cause.

There may be similar hazards associated with intensive farming. It is now fairly common practice to control the date of birth of farm animals, especially sheep. The ewes are treated with hormones to bring them all into season simultaneously so

162

that they can be batch mated and the whole flock will produce lambs at the same time.

They may even be induced to produce an extra crop a year. The dangers to humans caused by handling the hormones to do this may not yet be fully understood.

Racehorse stable boys recently reported an unaccustomed state of impotence and perhaps it is no coincidence that it is common to encourage mares to foal early in the year because they are entered for races not by the month of their birth, but the year.

I do not think men who organised European Conservation Year are the cranks they may seem. If we do not protect wild-life from the hazards of progress, we may be the next on the list of casualties ourselves.

53. Animal play school

March 6, 1970

We haven't had much snow for years, but I waited till March to say so because I didn't want to tempt providence. Now look what has happened! Still, quite heavy falls from now on are not likely to last long because the sun gets a little stronger every day.

This year, our blacksmith made me a rough triangular steel bracket to fit the back of my old tractor and I bolted a great oak plank, 10 ft long, onto it. When the weather broke, I played with it like a kid with a toboggan, clearing the snow from the yard and a quarter-mile down the drive to the farm below us.

What used to be a back-breaking chore with shovel and yard broom was suddenly transformed into a delightful game. And as the blacksmith only charged me thirty bob for the bracket, it was pleasure bought cheaply.

Meanwhile, the dogs have had their fun even cheaper. It has cost them nothing but the energy to skim round in circles and parabolas and curves. With the possible exception of cheetahs, I know nothing which moves with more grace than a lurcher bitch in the prime of condition. She has almost the speed of a greyhound, but the cross of sheepdog in her ancestry gives her far greater cunning and the finesse to control direction delicately.

Our three, Spider, Fly and Mandy, went round the paddock twisting and turning with no discernible pattern to their movements. One second they were a hundred yards apart and the next they converged on precisely the same spot so that catastrophic collision seemed inevitable. They maintained perfect control simply by using their tails like rudders to shift their balance slightly as they leaned at impossible angles to change direction.

As they approached each other, they writhed their lips in mock fury, as if each would tear out the other's throat. But before their jaws had time to snap, their speed had drifted them yards apart again. It was spectacular lilting motion and the only sound was the background of their breathing and the faint sibilance as they kicked up flurries of powdered snow.

Animals play more than men and the sensual pleasure their games provide is closely linked with their way of life. Dogs are hunting animals which would have to catch their prey to live in the wild. So my lurchers instinctively choose the catch-as-catch-can type of games which get them fit and give them practice, not only in covering ground quickly but in shifting direction accurately.

Dogs are also pack animals, psychologically attuned to obeying a pack leader who is chosen, not because he is right, but because of his might; because he is stronger and braver and can fight more effectively than the subservient members of the pack. So dogs play aggressive games from puppyhood. They bare their teeth so that they can bite their opponents without damaging their own sensitive lips.

They snarl and growl like tub-thumping speakers to demoralise all within earshot before ever a blow is struck. They acquire the exact timing to knock an opponent off his feet and lay bare his vulnerable throat. Because they are designed to live in packs subject to the discipline of a pack leader, the best and happiest dogs have masters who control them, not owners who spoil them.

Play is as universal among wild animals as tame – and just as indicative of their character. A litter of wild stoats will tumble over the ground in a turbulent ball of mock-attack, training themselves to kill before they leave their mother's teats. They somersault in an ageless dance which, despite its beauty, was designed by Nature to mesmerise their prey long enough for them to get within striking distance.

Our roe deer come out of the wood to graze at dusk and suddenly explode from peace to madness. They dash along the edge of the pool and over the mound where the badger sett is and into the wood. We watch them with baited breath because they weave in and out of the trees so recklessly that the slightest slip seems certain to break their necks. Out of the wood they come into the open and across the paddock and round the pool into the spinney again. They are seized with blind panic which will not release them till they drop exhausted, but the cause of their fear is never overcome.

This is because they are not really frightened at all. Their mad race is as much a game as the beautiful rhythm of the lurchers, but, instead of the instinctive dance of the hunter, this is the dance of the hunted. They are not practising capturing their prey, they are practising escape from their enemies.

They run full tilt in and out among the trees until they know every inch of their territory by heart. Less experienced pursuers following would run the risk of annihilation.

Our own childish games reveal human instincts almost as clearly. Follow-my-leader and wrestling, children's love of guns and the primitive urge to play with fire and water, all have their parallels in nature.

The mass hysteria so easily produced in crowds and the anarchy of violent demonstrations are symptoms of pack mentality without the discipline of a pack leader.

It is easy to flatter ourselves that civilisation has brought us far from primitive man, but comparison with the behaviour of the animals we see every day might show how scratch-deep our culture really is.

54. *Animals like the soft urban life*

March 13, 1970

I loathed almost every hour I spent in London as a student. No place on earth seemed as cold and inhospitable as London streets whipped by a March east wind. Nowhere was as stuffy as the same streets, sweating it out in a heatwave.

So it seemed all the more strange to see wood pigeons feeding fearlessly on the grubby little lawn of my London digs. Wood pigeons are among the shyest and most wary birds that ever scrumped a farmer's crops. They have to because every man's hand is against them in the country.

Sportsmen from towns dress up in Sherlock Holmes hats to creep up on them with the stealth of deer stalkers. Farm workers go out at dusk and blaze away at them as they come unsuspecting to their roost. Professional pigeon shooters seduce them with painted decoys and the Ministry of Agriculture concocts recipes of poisoned bait to add to their diet sheet.

Small wonder that these bashful birds melt over the horizon when their sharp eyes spot a human being. Perhaps the cockney birds at my digs had drawn courage from the brash house sparrows that do not give a damn for danger, but dive fearlessly in wherever there is food to be had.

Whatever the cause of the wood pigeons' unnatural boldness, I felt that I had much to learn from it. They had adapted to urban conditions while I could not. Wood pigeons and sparrows have no monopoly of this flair for improvisation. Jays and magpies and grey squirrels are more commonly seen on city bird tables than they are in the heart of well-keepered country.

A naturalist friend of mine saw so many foxes in the suburbs of Bristol that he organised a party of fellow enthusiasts to patrol a careful route he chose to get a comprehensive census. They motored round quiet streets at four o'clock in the morning, taking careful note of every fox they saw. Their tally ran into the teens, not of grinning masks in glass cases, but of living statistics, filed for future reference.

This creep of foxes into towns is nothing new. When I lived

in Bloxwich, a vixen had her annual litter of cubs under a summerhouse behind the Stafford Road. And a policeman in Dudley told me that he had been standing quietly in a shop doorway in the small hours of the morning, when there was a shattering noise in the darkness a few yards along the pavement. The beam of his torch did not pick out a saboteur on the wrong end of his time bomb, nor a gang of smash-and-grabbers. It floodlit a fox in the act of tipping the lids off a row of dustbins in search of tasty garbage.

Foxes will eat almost anything from the grapes of Aesop's fable to the rottenest stinking carrion, a craving for high game which was nearly the downfall of a fox in one Walsall garden.

The unwilling hostess was a pillar of the local animal protection society. Her beloved pet dog had died and been decently buried beneath a memorial patch of flowers in the garden. Several weeks later, just as the pangs of parting were beginning to dull, it seemed that an earthquake had hit the flower bed. The culprit was no human vandal. A fox had noticed an appetising aroma of 'game' percolating through the new-turned soil and helped himself to supper.

Countrymen often regard foxes as high class hunters who would spurn anything less than the fattest pheasant or poultry of unimpeachable pedigree. But town foxes are scavengers and carrion eaters with tastes as low as jackals.

They have discovered an easy living in city streets where men can't shoot them, even if they want, and where foxhounds would kill more pet cats than wild foxes. They have joined the band of magpies and crows and jays, which take easy picking by living on their wits.

Some creatures use towns only as dormitories. Instead of working in towns and commuting at night to the country, as humans do, they reverse the process. Birmingham starlings are a good example. They congregate by the thousand in the city centre as dusk falls every night, and annoy the inhabitants by fouling window ledges and roofs and gutters – and any pedestrians who do not take effective evasive action.

Some of them, I suppose. feed by day on the scraps thrown out by housewives or delve for grubs in city gardens. But the majority must fly for miles into the surrounding countryside to forage. Why then should they bother to fly back to their grimy roost at night? Why do they not roost in great flocks in pleasant woodland nearer to their source of food? The woods after all are the places they would naturally choose, for their country cousins sometimes smother trees so densely that their droppings poison the roots and kill them.

Collared doves, the latest avian immigrants to colonise England, prefer town to country life and grey squirrels are more common in Edgbaston than in isolated woodland.

But the most astonishing birds to hanker after human habitation are the swifts that arrive with the late spring. They are larger than swallows or house martins and fly higher and faster. Their aerobatics are so superb that some say they even sleep on the wing.

Just the birds, you might say, to revel in Nature's wildest solitudes. But you would be wrong. Swifts are town birds, nesting under the eaves of high buildings. Their high pitched cries of ecstasy have earned them the Black Country name of Jack Squallers and squadrons of them imprinted on my ears my few happy memories of my prep school in Edgbaston.

There are swifts in the village a mile away from me, but nothing I can do has convinced them that my way of life is best. They prefer the city lights (or at least life in the village) to being buried with me in the country.

55. Joe's eyes ease the journey

April 3, 1970

The bleak prospect of 300 miles in the confinement of my car was scarcely enriched by an isolated hitch-hiker thumbing a lift. The last time I had been caught was by a long-haired student wearing a chip on his shoulder as big as a chapel. His wispy beard was the only obvious indication of his sex, and he suffered under the contradictory delusions that the world owed him a living and Chairman Mao was tops. It was plain to the dullest human senses that he thought washing effete so I stopped the car and tipped him out again.

Being unwilling to repeat the experience, I eyed my prospective passenger more warily this time. He was in his twenties, had a short-back-and-sides, and an unfashionable air of normality. I soon discovered that his name was Joe, his home was in Birmingham and that he had spent several years selling vending machines. Then he had decided to do something more worthwhile than filling factory tea mugs.

Although he had no 'A' levels, he had sold himself to a Welsh university where he was playing Rugby football and hoping to qualify as a clinical psychologist. Joe was hitching back after watching an international rugger match and I was returning from the Mammal Society conference which was in Edinburgh this year, so I looked forward to seeing the country through his eyes.

Our first point of difference was about the scenery. He thought that the golden russet valleys which rolled up to the snow capped hills were very romantic. He loved the rugged grandeur, where granite rocks cropped out, and the scudding grey clouds reminded him of the swirling music of bagpipes.

I found the valleys golden, not with riches, but with inhospitable feggy grass. Proof of that pudding was in the number of animals grazing there. They could be counted as acres to the sheep instead of sheep to our more productive southern acre. Counting them would not have cured the mildest insomnia. The kindest colour to my eyes was the rich brown new-ploughed soil with its promise of plenty at harvest. It was so soft and friable that I longed for the sensuous pleasure of feeling it crumble through my fingers.

We both agreed about the stone walls, which snaked in slinky patterns down to the rivers and up the hills and over the skyline beyond. They were beautifully fashioned; monuments to the craftsmen who laboured to build them, the winds hissed through their crevices in a lament which made Joe's swirling bagpipes sound tame by comparison.

For the first twenty or thirty miles outside Edinburgh, every tiny cottage wore an air of prosperity. Each little garden was planted and window frames and wicket gates were brightly painted. There were roses up and down each rustic door and the lawns had been trimmed by machine instead of being bitten bare by hungry sheep.

These were not signs of wealth of a healthy agricultural community but the success symbols of mechanised commuters. Isolated cottages which could have been picked up for £50 after the war are now worth £1,000 or more – so long as they are close enough to a city for their owners to drive to work each day. Shrewd businessmen have grown rich by buying derelict heaps for a fistful of fivers and flogging them for a fortune when the motorway comes by five years later.

The original owners are often happy enough to swap their ruin with no damp course, no bus, no shop, no piped water and an earth closet, for a council house in the village with all mod cons. Newcomers either have the brass to remedy such defects or, if not, convince themselves that they are 'quaint' and 'desirable'.

But we disagreed about cutting the motorway through farms and large estates. We went through several which must have looked out over rolling parkland or fertile fields and belonged to the same families for generations. Their owners must have seen the same scene and employed the same families for so long that their hereditary love of the place would grow as deep as the roots of their trees.

Then, however hard they fought, the motorway split their land from them. To me, it had the pathos of men dispossessed by war. Joe acknowledged it 'must have annoyed them a bit', but he was far more concerned that privilege had made way for progress.

We agreed again about the despoliation of the Lake District. When it was relatively inaccessible, it had the priceless charm of solitude. The crags and fells were so remote that they cradled the atmosphere of escape. Now that it is possible to arrive in about three hours from the thronging Midlands, the roads are as cluttered there on Sunday afternoons as Evesham in blossom time or Cheltenham on race days.

Half the fun of that ride with Joe was the different things we saw. It had never occurred to him what a lot of molehills there are this year or how many kestrel hawks hunt the verges of motorways. And he had not appreciated that different breeds of cattle have been carefully evolved to suit different soils and conditions. Highland cattle with shaggy coats to withstand the hard weather but still do well on poor pasture. Herefords and sleek black Aberdeen Angus which produce the best beef in the world.

I spotted the hares sitting out on the ploughland and he noticed the gleamiest Mercedes and the latest model Bentleys. He had an eye for architecture and pointed out the modern idiom (as he called it) while I hankered after the security implied by antiquity.

We laughed and argued and agreed all the way from Edinburgh to the turn for Chester where he hoped to hitch another lift.

56. Polishing the keeper's image

April 10, 1970

The first impression of the little cottage in the wood might well have been that it was the most peaceful spot on earth. I used to go there soon after the First World War when aeroplanes were still a rarity, and there was no mechanical sound to disturb the solitude. The wood nestled in the midst of hundreds of acres of rolling parkland where only cattle grazed and the stillness was broken by nothing but the song of birds.

As you walked towards it, along a winding path of gay rhododendrons, there was always a rabbit or two bobbing about in the bushes, pheasants by the score, and the drone of wood pigeons.

The walls of that cottage parlour were lined with glass cases full of stuffed foxes and owls, white stoats and small birds of every description. There was even a kingfisher, I remember, very badly stuffed, holding in its bill what looked like a petrified sardine. A sandy badger glared at an albino pheasant, and there were racks of shining guns and handcuffs and boxes and boxes of cartridges.

It never occurred to my boyish imagination what a contrast this armoury of weapons and museum trophies was to the peace and quiet outside. I was far too lost in admiration for the spaniels and retrievers in their kennels by the backdoor to notice unpleasant things and I envied the life of the gamekeeper who lived there.

Even his gibbet impressed me, not by its pathos, but by its proof of the skill which had so festooned it with death. There were always a few carrion crows nailed on display and jays whose feathers dulled as time weathered their gaudy plumage. Casual inspection revealed that stoats and weasels, hawks and magpies, and badgers and owls were foolish to be deluded by the peaceful atmosphere of that wood.

Although it never dawned on me at the time, the most significant clue was not outside, but in the cottage parlour. An enormous tabby cat was tethered by a lead where he could curl in comfort by the fire. He was the only cat I have ever seen wearing a collar and chain. If he had broken loose, he would have suffered the dreadful fate of all cats who trespassed there and were caught by the leg in a steel gintrap.

In those days, a keeper's worth was calculated by the amount of vermin that he could kill. He displayed this with pride on his gibbet, and he regarded every bird with a hooked bill and every animal with canine teeth as his sworn enemies. If he saw a strange or exceptionally beautiful bird or animal, his instinct was not to preserve it, so that its kind could multiply, but to shoot it and stuff it in a case.

There have been keepers like that for the last two centuries – and there are still keepers like that today. Thy have, of course, to be more discreet about what adorns their gibbets, because of modern bird protection laws, but a bad keeper can still wreak havoc in the inviolable privacy of his beat.

Mr Brown is different. He is head keeper to the Earl of Aylesford at Packington, in Warwickshire, and he combines being a good keeper with being a good naturalist. He told me, with great pride this week, that he has a pair of buzzards resident on his beat and that badgers are as safe with him as pheasants.

Snow geese and glaucous gulls – both rarities in the Midlands – have delighted him this winter; not stuffed in glass cases, but alive and well on the lakes.

Mr Brown must have done as much as anybody to give the modern keeper a less tarnished image. I met him about a decade ago at the first Gamekeepers' Fair. His employer, Lord Aylesford, told me at the time that they were organising a gamekeepers' fair on the estate and that he would 'try to get me a ticket'.

I asked him why he would have to try since the estate belonged to him, and he said that his head keeper, not he, was host and that invitations were going only to other keepers and a few personal friends. But he might be persuaded to add me to the list. As an event for gamekeepers, it aimed to be a social get-together rather than a commercially biased show like the Game Fair, which is run by the Country Landowners' Association.

That first Gamekeepers' Fair was a howling success. Each keeper invited could bring a guest. This could be his employer, if he wanted, but no employer could come if his keeper did not invite him!

There was clay pigeon shooting and gundog trials and a bar where employer-guests could buy their keeper-hosts a drink. The beauty was that since hosts had restricted guests to the people they wanted, everyone got on fine with everyone else.

The original idea was that a different head keeper on a different estate should be host each year. But hospitality at Packington was so lavish and Mr Brown was such a good host that nobody else wanted to compete. The result is that the Gamekeepers' Fair at Packington has become a national event on the annual sporting calendar and, inevitably, it has grown.

It is being held again tomorrow and admittance is no longer strictly by invitation. The general public can now get in and are welcomed to see for themselves the sort of methods modern keepers use. It has become so widely recognised that the Forestry Commission will be there with a demonstration of how to combine wildlife with forestry, and the Ministry of Agriculture will show how to control pests more humanely than the keeper did at the cottage of my youth.

There will be clay pigeon shooting and gundog competitions, fly casting demonstrations and trade stands. And, of course, a bar. Mr Brown will be there, as genial a host as ever, and so will his employer Lord Aylesford. I hope that, by the end of the day, they will have converted a few more die-hard shooting men to their way of thinking.

57. Perils of poisons, pesticides—and late spring

May 1, 1970

Keen ornithologists think nothing of going several hundred miles to see an osprey and they become ecstatic about any rare bird that honours our shores by a visit. They keep checklists as long as their arms, ticking off the species they see with the dedication of train spotters or collectors of Victorian matchbox lids.

This cult of rarity provides a powerful lobby to protect our threatened species but it is a form of avian snobbery which otherwise leaves me cold.

The song of a common blackbird in my own garden delights me quite as keenly as a nightingale on some southern heath and the blue tits squabbling on our bird table are as welcome as far-off feathered aristocrats.

The smallest town garden often has blackbirds nesting in the privet hedge, blue tits in the nesting box and robins by the compost heap. This year, I suspect, these birds in towns may well have done better than they would with us in deep country. It has been such a late spring that suitable cover is still as scarce as gold, and any nest in the country which is not properly concealed is almost certain to be robbed by jays or magpies or crows. And whatever the Bird Protection Acts say, village boys are still addicted to bird nesting.

Stanley Porter, who takes many bird photographs, has been watching the progress of an early nest of blackbirds in his garden in Moseley. Last year, they nested within two feet of his kitchen window, in the mass of honeysuckle which smothers his coal shed. He pulled out the old nest at the end of the season and they rewarded him by nesting again in exactly the same place this year.

It is usually worth pulling out old nests in winter because their debris may sterilise an otherwise desirable site next year. The nest may also be so lousy with hibernating parasites that next season's young would be eaten alive if the old birds did refurbish it.

Despite this cold spring, the four eggs hatched out by the Porters' kitchen window and chicks grew apace till they were eight days old. On the ninth morning, they were all dead.

A common cause of such disasters is that cats capture the old birds or they have some other accident, leaving the young to starve. Not so in this case. All the young birds died suddenly within the space of a few hours and since the parents had not deserted them, it is possible that their sudden death was due to poison. Many of the insecticides sold to gardeners wreak havoc on wildlife. This is the season when people are dressing their lawns for pests and the nestlings probably had poisoned insects for their breakfast.

I am glad to say that weedkillers and pesticides are now proving dangerous to human beings as well as to wildlife, so that there is at least some chance that they will be more rigorously controlled.

The instinct for reproduction proved such an irresistible urge that, within twenty-four hours of the nestlings' death, the old birds were building again. This time they have chosen a hawthorn tree about five yards away, so I wish them better luck with their second brood.

Our leaves are so late that birds have chosen some pretty bizarre nest sites in their efforts to skulk out of sight of predators. One thrush is sitting on four eggs in her nest, on the beam of the fowlpen, and there is a blackbirds' brood above the workbench in my garage.

Blue tits have occupied four nest boxes round the garden and the pied wagtails have taken the nest box by the kitchen window where they reared successfully the last two years.

I'm rather worried about the swallows and martins because a friend who lives down by the River Blythe was delighted to see his arrive – until he found some of them dead but unmarked. They do not seem to have been poisoned, so we think that our cold weather was too much for them while they were still weak from their long migration flight.

When we came to Goat Lodge six years ago, the whole area was very deficient in deep cover. The tops of the trees in the wood were dense enough, but the ground would have been safer if it had been carpeted with brambles. So we planted shrubs in the wood and a hedge of hawthorn down the side, and set about the garden.

We put a yew hedge down one side and a double hedge of hornbeam and rhododendron down the other. It is as important to provide nesting sites in summer as food on the bird table in winter.

We haven't been rewarded by anything very exciting so far this year – at least by the rarity culture's yardstick. But a pair of mistle thrushes have taken up residence in the yew tree, a blackbird in the yew hedge and a song thrush in a dense clump of bamboo.

An old mallard duck has tucked her nest away at the bottom of the same clump of bamboo and all the old birds were feeding on the lawn when we looked out of the window at first light this morning. When their chicks hatch out, they will have to keep their eyes skinned for crows and magpies, but at least they need have no worries that we shall poison their worms on the lawn.

58. The bird that out-taps a jazz drummer

May 15, 1970

Twice within the last few weeks I have been delighted to catch a glimpse of the lesser spotted woodpecker. It is the smallest of our native woodpeckers, little bigger than a starling. And I could count on my fingers the number of times I've seen one in our wood.

This is partly because it is fairly rare, but also because it is so shy and spends a great deal of its time flitting, with its undulating flight, from the top of one tree to the next.

Its black neck and wings are conspicuously barred with white, and the heads of the cock birds and the youngsters are crowned in beautiful crimson. Such a vivid splash of colour would seem impossible to miss against the dowdy trunks of trees. But once the leaf is on, it is all too easy to pass in ignorance within a few feet of these charming litle birds, and I have never been able to convince myself that they pay us more than fleeting visits.

We get quite a few green woodpeckers and last year a great spotted woodpecker brought off a brood of young in an ash tree within fifty yards of the house.

However secretive its smaller relative may be, there is no shadow of doubt when the great spotted (or pied) woodpecker sets up home. The whole wood resounds with its drumming which is produced by choosing a resonant hollow trunk and subjecting it to a fusillade of blows from the bird's chisel beak. So rapid is the tattoo that the most frenzied efforts of the slickest jazz drummer are Dead March tempo by comparison.

When the young hatch out, their appetites are insatiable and their manners deplorable. From dawn to dusk they advertise their presence by incessant squalls for food. The combination of bright plumage and the reckless row they make are pretty good indications that they need have little fear of enemies. The weaklings of the feathered world have to ensure their survival by being more discreet.

On top of this, the woodpeckers need fear competition for food no more than assault by predators. They avoid attack by making holes in trees where they can nest in safety, well away from larger creatures which might eat their young. Their food is mainly grubs and beetles, buried deep in rotten wood, far out of reach of other birds.

Countless centuries of evolution have helped each generation of most species to survive more efficiently than the last. Swifts and swallows have perfected superb feats of aerobatics, almost to the exclusion of their ability to walk. Meanwhile, the woodpecker tribe have learned to run up and down vertical tree trunks with the ease of acrobatic steeplejacks. Swallows have developed wide little beaks, to scoop up insects in full flight, while woodpecker's bills grew longer and stronger.

The most stupid members of the human race are said to bang their heads against the wall because it is so lovely when they stop. Woodpeckers have become so specialised that they can smack their bills into solid tree trunks without contracting so much as a headache.

Even so, they are wise enough to choose trees which are not impregnable. They like trees with pulpy hearts. They discover this by tapping the tree trunk and deducing from the notes their blows emit whether the wood is sound or whether the heart has started to decay.

This instinct for a soft touch is vital. Decaying wood is soon colonised by insects, and the moths and beetles lay eggs from which the larvae tunnel deep out of sight to feed in safety.

It gives a sense of security which proves illusory as soon as a woodpecker taps the surface of the tree for soundings. Dull and unresponsive trees ask for trouble, and the woodpecker's bill rattles on the trunk with the frequency of a pneumatic drill, leaving a pile of slivers at the foot of the tree. The hard shell soon splits off, exposing the soft decay inside, to deliver up its victims so that the woodpecker can gorge or fly off to feed its young.

It may seem an odd contradiction that the very efficiency which enables woodpeckers to tunnel into wood can be their undoing, for the advantages do not result in the population explosion you might expect. Woodpeckers are, in fact, getting rarer.

Cheeky starlings, far too small to harm the birds themselves, damage them by stealing their nesting tunnels. And although the woodpecker's bill is as strong as a hammer and chisel, it guards a tongue of exceptional length for winkling grubs from their holes. This tongue is so long and so delicate that it is extremely sensitive to frostbite and the farther north you go, the less chance you have of seeing woodpeckers.

It is strange that a bird with a bill powerful enough to tear its food from the heart of an oak should have a tongue so fragile that every hard winter threatens death from exposure.

59. Feathered shadow boxers

June 12, 1970

A reader from Water Orton wrote to me last week to ask about the 'very curious behaviour' of her local magpie. She said that for the last four or five weeks, the bird has been coming every morning, between 5 and 6.30 a.m. to a bird table about 4 ft from the window of her sun lounge. Then he launched himself at the window, giving it two hefty thuds, and returned to the bird table. He repeated this for about ten minutes and then flew away across the fields.

He always flies at the same pane, though others are equally accessible, but he ignores it if the curtains are drawn. Curiously enough exactly the same thing happened at the same time last year and always at an early hour in the morning. My correspondent says that there does not seem to be anything to attract a magpie inside the room, so what is my explanation?

Bouts of window bashing are quite common among many birds, though I think pied wagtails are the most common among such shadow boxers. I have never heard of it happening with a magpie before, because magpies are normally far too crafty and wary to be conned into a rough house which might turn out to be a trap.

The reader was probably quite right when she said there was nothing in the sun lounge to *attract* a magpie. My guess is that there was something there which it found utterly repulsive.

What he saw, from his aggressive vantage point, was a beautiful cock magpie, in all the arrogant virility of his breeding plumage. And he could not tolerate such a rival on his territory, especially at breeding time.

So he flew into the attack, to discover that the interloper became airborne with telepathic precision at exactly the same instant, so that they collided in mid-air half way between their respective launching pads. It didn't dawn on him that what he saw in the window was his own reflection, so he sailed into attacks to drive off such a cheeky trespasser.

This would explain why the bird buffeted only one pane of the window. From his perch on the bird table, his reflection always glowered back at him from precisely the same angle. It would also explain the fact that he took no notice when the curtains were drawn, because he would then seem but a pale shadow of himself, when there was no dark background to give him contrast.

The last two clues to be fitted into the jig-saw of this eccentric bird's behaviour both concern his punctuality. He bashed his head, if not against a brick wall, at least against unyielding panes of glass, not only at the same time each year (the breeding season) but even at the same time each day.

The time of day is also easy. First thing in the morning small birds are engrossed in nest building or feeding young which are famished by waiting for food through the hours of darkness. All the crows and magpies need to do then is to perch unseen and watch where their quarry is hidden.

Only avian fools go searching for nests when mums are driven so relentlessly to feed their insatiable young that their careless devotion shows robbers where to go. So hungry magpies hang around at dawn, whetting their appetites with the prospect that their victims will blaze the trails to their eating places as clearly as if they lighted them with neon signs.

Human beings often have so little faith in their own judgement that they do not believe any eating place can be good unless they are practically trodden underfoot in the rush to get there. Birds are not so stupid. When magpies have picked a territory which oozes with protein-rich birds' eggs and screams with succulent fledglings simply asking to be gobbled up, they try to keep it to themselves.

If any rival comes in sight, the 'owner' of the territory sees him off, first by a swaggering threat display. This isn't all bombast. Might is right in their world, and if a string of chattering abuse does not do the trick, any cock magpie worth his salt will soon back up his boasts.

Not having been introduced to scientific devices, like mirrors, the Water Orton bird can be forgiven for believing that the bird he saw through the sun lounge window was a stranger. When he flew headlong at him, he must have thought not only that he packed a hefty punch, but was disconcertingly eager to come back for more.

The first time I came across similar behaviour was at a fishing hotel in Wales. We didn't go for the fishing, but for the wild country and the variety of bird life we found along the river there. The morning we arrived we noticed a dirty patch in the bottom corner of the bar window and, within minutes, the cause was obvious.

It was a pugilistic pied wagtail, knocking the hell out of the reflection he saw from the window sill. He battered the bloom from his feathers on the unrelenting glass and, when he dropped to the ground exhausted, he obviously thought that the fact that he could no longer see his rival meant that he had won!

So certain was he that he flew off round the back of the hotel looking for the vanquished at the tradesmen's entrance. That illusion of victory must have been a marvellous feeling. Within seconds he was back, triumphant, to tell the world that he had won and that his foe was only a big-mouthed coward who wouldn't stop to swap real punishment.

But when he jumped back to his perch on the window sill to boast of his feats to the crowd in the bar – there was his enemy glaring from the window as perky as ever. So the whole drama was re-enacted again and again, sapping his strength and knocking the gloss off his plumage, but never convincing him how hollow most victories really prove to be.

60. *In search of the perfect companion*

June 19, 1970

Favourite dogs have always filled a large part of my life. Mick was the first, and he arrived as a pot-bellied little whelp when I was eight years old and he was eight weeks. His mother was a fox terrier, and if his looks were anything to go by, she had taken more than a passing fancy to a Stafford Bull Terrier that lived down the street.

Mick grew up with the powerful chest and fierce expression of a fighting dog, set on hindquarters too little for his size. He slept in my room at night and was a shadow at my heels all day until he died eleven years later. He filled my lonely childhood with happy memories and he gave me the taste for ratting and rabbitting which grew into a far wider love of country things.

Mick was followed by two Stafford Bull Terriers, Grip and Rebel. Rebel was a white bitch with a fawn patch on her head, who became widely famous for her skill in catching rats. I basked in her reflected glory because folk, who didn't know my name, referred to me as ' 'im as belongs to the lemon-eyed bitch'.

Then came Dinah, a gentle little cross between a whippet and a terrier, who lasted fourteen years, and Tough my Alsatian who was poisoned last autumn.

She was such a good dog that I have been trying to get another Alsatian to replace her ever since. I have answered dozens of advertisements and seen literally scores of puppies, but Alsatians have become a 'popular' breed and some people breed them only for profit.

In common with other breeds which dog shows have made popular, some Alsatians now have hereditary defects. A high-ranking police officer finally put me off by telling me the number which had to be destroyed because they developed hip dysplasia, an in-bred deformity of the hind quarters.

So I turned my attention to 'working' breeds, whose value is assessed by the deeds they perform instead of their looks, and I finally settled for a German Short-haired Pointer. These were evolved with Teutonic thoroughness as all-round gun dogs to help sportsmen in the field.

They have superb noses to hunt for their quarry. When they find it, they 'freeze' like statues to show their master where it hides. When he flushes it out and it is shot, they gently retrieve it.

Such practical sportsmen do not waste time on weaklings with wobbly knees, nor heavy creatures that are frightened of their shadows. If their puppies are not bold and intelligent and physically fit, they do not waste time rearing them. It is a doctrine with which I entirely agree.

At last I have run my ideal puppy to ground. A friend who is an internationally famous field trial judge, introduced me to the secretary of the breed society. He, in turn, gave me a list of the owners who kept the sort of dog I wanted.

The trail led me to a chalet by the river at Stourport-on-Severn, where I found a beautiful pointer bitch sunning herself on the turf, and six puppies, seven weeks old, rolling and gambolling around her.

Their owner was a man after my own heart. Having served his time in the army, he had no wish to get involved in the rat race of civvy street. So he bought a little business which catered for his simple needs with two hard days' work a week. He spent the other five wandering by the river and in the green fields around it, messing about, with his dog.

A six-year-old, this bitch had just had her second litter. Before he would even begin to discuss price – which turned out to be about half what other breeders asked – he needed the assurance that his pup would go to a good home, to a master who would use it and not keep it as an ornament.

I brought the pick of the litter back with me. She is a little bitch with a liver-coloured head and grey body, ticked with liver spots. Within two days, she answered to her name of Tick and by the third day she would sit on command.

When I introduced her to Mandy, Spider and Fly, the lurchers, she thought they were far too large for comfort. But she wasn't frightened of them. She guarded her rear and flanks by taking refuge between my feet, writhed back her lips and snarled her gusty defiance at them. Since then, she has been their boss.

When Miss Roedoe, my tame deer, came to investigate the newcomer, Tick 'pointed' at her in case I hadn't seen a deer before. And when she came into the garden, she lopped off the heads of my wife's choice flowers – just in case they turned out to be weeds.

It may seem strange for a naturalist to choose for his bosom companion, a dog evolved by shooting men. But I have always had the highest respect for the ruthless selection that produces tough dogs, which can think instead of being baubles held on the end of leads.

If shooting men can train dogs like mine to 'point' pheasants and partridges for their sport, I can train Tick to show me all sorts of creatures which would otherwise have remained concealed as I passed them by. She should be the ideal companion for country walks, to show me things undiscovered by dull human senses.

We have already struck up a friendship. She is curled asleep at my feet as I write this, and when I have done, she will come for a walk with the other dogs and me in the wood. For the next ten to fifteen years, with luck, she will welcome my friends and see off my foes, and share my joys of wandering alone in quiet places.

It is already obvious that she is one of the most intelligent pups I have ever had. I hope that she will live to join the handful of 'favourite' dogs which have spanned my life.

Index